W9-DAU-079

Livonia Public Library
ALFRED NOBLE BRANCH
32901 PLYMOUTH ROAD
Livonia, Michigan 48150
421-6600

ISLE ROYALE

SHIPWRECKS

Copyright 1983

ISBN 0-932212-08-5
Library of Congress No. 82-74365

By Frederick Stonehouse & Avery Color Studios
Marquette, Michigan   AuTrain, Michigan

Published by
Avery Color Studios
AuTrain, Michigan 49806

First Edition - February 1983
Reprinted - 1983, 1986, 1987, 1989

No portion of this publication may be reproduced, reprinted or otherwise copied for distribution purposes
without the express written permission of the author and
publisher.

Livonia Public Library
ALFRED NOBLE BRANCH
32901 PLYMOUTH ROAD
Livonia, Michigan 48150
421-6600

3 9082 02077286 2

MAY 1 0 1990

TABLE OF CONTENTS

ACKNOWLEDGEMENTS

I would like to thank the following people and institutions for their very kind efforts on my behalf. Producing a book like "Isle Royale Shipwrecks" is not a one-man project. It required active help and assistance from many people. I am deeply appreciative of their aid.

Mr. Thomas E. Appleton, Historian of the Canadian Coast Guard

Rev. Edward J. Dowling, S.J.

Jean Haviland

Janice L. Haas of the Rutherford B. Hayes Library, Fremont, Ohio

C. Patrick Labadie of the Lake Superior Marine Museum, Duluth, Minnesota

Robert E. Lee of the Great Lakes Maritime Institute, Detroit, Michigan

Marsha Lessun of the Northern Michigan University Olson Library, Marquette, Michigan

Ruth Revels and Paul Woehrmann of the Milwaukee Public Library

William F. Sherman, Hope K. Holdcamper, Janet L. Hargett, Kenneth R. Hall and Joel Barker of the National Archives, Washington, D.C.

Elaine Thorsen and the staff of the Peter White Public Library, Marquette, Michigan

Brian Hallett of the Public Archives of Canada

Kenneth E. Thro

Jean Olson

The Canada Steamship Lines

The Canadian Pacific Railroad

The Great Lakes Historical Society, Vermilion, Ohio

McGill University's McCord Museum

The Marquette County Historical Society, Marquette, Michigan

The Michigan Technological University Archives, Houghton, Michigan

The National Maritime Museum, Greenwich, England

The Queens University Archives, Canada

INTRODUCTION

If you are fortunate enough to read this book while on Isle Royale, don't miss the opportunity to actually visit the areas at which the wrecks occurred. Lookout Louise is an especially good vantage point. From its heights, you look down upon the jagged reefs known as Canoe Rocks. With a pinch of imagination you can visualize the mighty steamer EMPEROR roaring down on them during the early morning darkness, impaling herself and dying in dreadful agony. The observer can also visualize the DUNELM stranding herself during the 1910 blizzard or the proud MONARCH cruising blindly past in 1906, only to meet her end at the base of the rock palisades south of Blake Point.

Little imagination is required to visualize the wreck of the CHESTER A. CONGDON, broken and sinking on the shoal just south of Canoe Rocks. Walk the beach opposite the ALGOMA wreck and imagine the horror of that terrible November night. Cruise over the sunken AMERICA and peer into the crystal depths. Try to catch a glimpse of the lonely Rock of Ages Light and picture the GEORGE M. COX high out of the water.

In short, take the opportunity to experience, through your imagination, the true meaning of the word "shipwreck." Put yourself in the place of sailors who manned the lost ships. Try to see what they saw. Feel what they felt. If you can, you will have gained some understanding of what shipwreck on Isle Royale and Lake Superior was all about.

This booklet is not a "definitive study" of the shipwrecks of Isle Royale. Rather, it is a survey of those wrecks which I feel are of major interest. The information contained in each story is as accurate as the sources from which it was drawn. The sources are listed after each story should the reader desire to pursue the tale further. There are varying accounts concerning several of the wrecks. In these instances I have used the one I consider most likely to be correct.

I have largely ignored the "I remember when" tales related by oldtimers who claim to have been present during a particular event. Although such oral history is presently very much in vogue, I strongly question its accuracy. As an historian, I have found such accounts entertaining, but of little practical value.

In terms of an overview of Lake Superior shipping history, Isle Royale is largely unimportant. Other than some relatively minor activity with copper mining, furs and fishing, lake commerce was sparse.

The question of why numerous wrecks occurred at Isle Royale is worthy of comment then.

With the exception of the CENTURION, HENRY CHISHOLM and AMERICA, the wrecks occurred to vessels attempting to simply avoid the island!

Many of the vessels (ALGOMA, CONGDON, MONARCH, EMPEROR, COX and KAMLOOPS) were either upbound or downbound from Thunder Bay and the elements simply forced them into contact with the island. Other vessels (TREVOR, ROCKEFELLER, BRANSFORD), were bound elsewhere, but met the island at the whim of the storm king.

Summed up differently, Isle Royale is a massvie menace to navigation. Remember, most of the lost vessels weren't seeking out Isle Royale landfalls; their only desire was to safely clear the island.

Strangely, Isle Royale is of more interest to Lake Superior maritime historians. Countless vessels passed her in safety, but a few didn't. Her wrecks are a veritable treasure trove of the maritime past.

The GEORGE M. COX and AMERICA are examples of a class of passenger vessel long gone from the Lake Superior scene. The ALGOMA, The HENRY CHISHOLM, CUMBERLAND and MONARCH are others. The EM-

PEROR and CONGDON were mere bulk freighters, but they still hold a special flavor all their own. Though only a scuba diver can explore these vessels, they provide unique insight into the maritime past of the greatest freshwater lake in the world.

— A rough appreciation of Isle Royale's position in the scheme of Lake Superior shipwrecks can be gained when the reader realizes that of an estimated 550 major wrecks in the lake, only about 25 occurred in the Isle Royale vicinity. Whitefish Point can lay claim to at least 60, the Grand Island area to 25 and Grand Marais to more than 40. In these examples, the definition of "major wreck" may be open to question, but the results, in terms of a general ratio of comparison, are not.

Regardless of the number of wrecks, to the diving historian, the shipwrecks of Isle Royale represent an important portion of the maritime history of Lake Superior.

MAPLE LEAF

One of the earliest schooners that scraped with Isle Royale was the brand new MAPLE LEAF. Upbound from Chicago for Duluth in October 1872, the schooner was driven ashore during a gale somewhere on the islands south coast. Probably the schooner was trying to seek shelter behind the island.

Reportedly, she was badly battered, losing her sails, rigging, masts and cabin. Her crew was rescued. Although it was originally thought the MAPLE LEAF was unsalvageable, quick work saved the schooner, but extensive repairs were required.

The schooner sailed for another ten years, until November 1882 when she was driven ashore near the mouth of Michigan's Iron River. This time salvage was impossible and she was a total loss of $3,000. Built at Bayfield, she was owned by R.D. Pike.

BIBLIOGRAPHY

Mansfield, John B., "HISTORY OF THE GREAT LAKES, VOL. 1" Chicago: J.H. Beers, 1899.

"MARQUETTE MINING JOURNAL." October 26, 1872, October 21, 1882.

"PORTAGE LAKE MINING GAZETTE" (Houghton). November 27, 1873

THE 'CUMBERLAND'
OF CUMBERLAND POINT

The oldest wreck on Isle Royale that historians are certain of, and divers can actually locate the wreckage of, is that of the Canadian passenger and freight steamboat CUMBERLAND.

The sidewheeler CUMBERLAND. Notice the "walking beam" of her steam engine protruding above her side-wheel.

Mariners Museum

The 418 ton CUMBERLAND, reportedly a fine-looking sidewheeler, was built in 1871 at Port Robinson, Ontario by Melancthon Simpson at a cost of $101,000. Owned by the Lake Superior Navigation Company, she was 204.5 feet in length, 26 feet in width and 10.7 feet in depth. Her power was provided by a huge, wheezing walking beam engine originally salvaged from the old paddlewheeler CATARACT built in 1847. The engine, a product of the Dunham Company of New York, had a 44 inch diameter piston with a 132 inch stroke.

As a typical vessel in the Lake Superior passenger and freight trade, she carried a wide assortment of cargos. An examination of the records at the St. Mary's Falls Ship Canal (today Soo Locks) shows her hold was usually filled with everything from barrelled flour, pork, butter, apples, coffee, tobacco, nails, shingles, hay, cattle and liquor. All were important staples to the early settlers of the rugged Lake Superior north shore region, the normal territory serviced by the steamer. The steamer was named for Fred W. Cumberland, the manager of the Northern Railway, the parent company of the shipping line.

The CUMBERLAND apparently had a fair first season, but ran into trouble in 1872 when she froze in the ice on the Georgian Bay's north shore. Earlier that year the CUMBERLAND rendered aid to the steamer MANITOBA when she found her stranded on a reef near Michipicoten Island in eastern Lake Superior. After removing the MANITOBA's 75 passengers, the CUMBERLAND pulled her free. Such mutual assistance was commonplace during the early days of lake sailing. 1873 passed without special problems, but in 1874 she was badly ravaged by a vicious Lake Superior October gale. Her difficulty could well have been caused by being somewhat overloaded since only after jettisoning part of her cargo was she able to struggle to safety at Prince Arthur's Landing (today's Port Arthur) where she promptly sank at the dock! The "working" of the vessel in the storm had loosened her caulking and her pumps couldn't handle the resulting leaking. The problem of a vessel "spitting" her caulking in a storm was not uncommon, and resulted in numerous losses.

Her owners quickly raised the CUMBERLAND and she ran without reported troubles for the next two years. It was the third year, however, that would be her undoing!

The final chain of circumstances leading to her loss began sometime around July 20 when she ran aground on

13

a reef in Nipigon Harbor on the Lake's north shore. She apparently suffered some fairly serious damage since she reportedly had four to six feet of water in her hold. It took three days for the CUMBERLAND to work herself off.

Free of the bar, the CUMBERLAND reached Prince Arthur's landing on the 24th where she quickly transferred her freight and passengers and rapidly left for Duluth.

It was while bound for Duluth that the CUMBERLAND plowed into Isle Royale's Rock of Ages Reef! She must have been steaming along at a pretty good clip, since it was reportedly that all of her forward half was hard on the reef. It was also reported that had she been 100 feet to the left, she would have been in safe water. The actual depth of water at the point she struck the reef was a mere six feet!

Why the CUMBERLAND struck the reef in what was evidently clear weather isn't known, but at the time it was suspected that the Captain had used Canadian charts which did not indicate the reef! Comparable U.S. Lake survey charts did indicate the reef.

Although several tugs did try to pull the CUMBERLAND off her perch, it was to no avail. Another side-wheeler, the 461 ton FRANCES SMITH, removed the CUMBERLAND's crew. On August 6, the wreckers gave up their efforts and her registry was closed on August 24. She was a loss of $50,000. Her short life had indeed been a rough one.

Struck as she was on an open reef without substantial weather protection from any direction, it can be surmised that fall and winter gales made short work of destroying the CUMBERLAND! When much of her wreckage drifted ashore on Isle Royale, the area was promptly tagged as "Cumberland Point."

Much of the wreckage of the CUMBERLAND is, however, still in the area of the reef. In the watery depths some of her ribbing and planking, as well as part of a paddle wheel can still be located. No part of the engine has been found which strongly suggests that the wreck-

14

ing company was at the vessel long enough to remove
much of her machinery and valuable equipment.

BIBLIOGRAPHY

*Benjamin Chynoweth Collection, Michigan Technological University,
Houghton, Michigan.*

*Charlebois, Dr. Peter. "STERNWHEELERS & SIDEWHEELERS, THE
ROMANCE OF STEAMDRIVEN PADDLE-BOATS IS CANADA,"
Toronto: NC Press Limited. 1978.*

"DULUTH MINNESOTIAN," August 4, 11, September 8, 1877.

*Holden, Thom. "Reef of the Three C's: Parts I - II," "THE NOR'EAST-
ER," July - August, 1977, March - April 1978.*

Mansfield, J.B. "HISTORY OF THE GREAT LAKES," Chicago, 1899.

*Michigan State Archives. "STATEMENT OF ARTICLES PASSING
THROUGH ST. MARY'S FALLS SHIP CANAL," November 12, December 31, 1871.*

*Mills, John M. "CANADIAN COASTAL AND INLAND STEAM VES-
SELS 1809 - 1930. Providence, Rhode Island: Steamship Historical
Society of America, 1979.*

Runge Collection, Milwaukee Public Library.

*Williams, W.R. "Shipwrecks at Isle Royale," "INLAND SEAS," winter
1956, p. 252.*

*Wolff, Julius F. "Canadian Shipwrecks of Lake Superior," "INLAND
SEAS," spring 1978, p. 38.*

*Young, Anna G. "GREAT LAKES SAGA," Owen Sound: Richardson,
Bond & Wright, Ltd. 1968.*

ALICE CRAIG

Commercial fishing has long been an activity on the island, and as might be expected, the vessels that engaged in it found themselves in a spot of trouble. One such vessel was the small schooner ALICE CRAIG.

On Sunday, October 12, 1884, the ALICE CRAIG was carrying a fish cargo when, buffeted by snow and gusting wind, she sailed onto the rocks at the northeast end of Menagerie Island.

Unable to free the schooner, the crew, with the help of the Menagerie Island lightkeeper, transferred her cargo to the island for safety. Later the steamer ISLE ROYALE tried to pull her free, but without success. When the ISLE ROYALE reached Port Arthur, she called to Bayfield for a tug.

The following Saturday, the small tug FAVORITE arrived from Bayfield. After a short pull, the tug had the schooner free. Soon after she towed her to Duluth for a drydocking and fairly extensive repairs.

The ALICE CRAIG was no stranger to trouble. Earlier in November of 1873 the CRAIG, together with two other schooners and a propeller, was blown on the beach at Duluth by a terrific storm.

BIBLIOGRAPHY

"BAYFIELD COUNTY PRESS." October 18 - November 1, 1884.
Kaups, Matti. "North Shore Commercial Fishing, 1849 - 1870." "MINNESOTA HISTORY."
"LOG OF THE LIGHT STATION AT MENAGERIE ISLAND." October 1884.
"MARQUETTE MINING JOURNAL." November 16, 23, 1872.
"RUNGE COLLECTION." Marine Room, Milwaukee Public Library.

ISLE ROYALE

The loss of the small steamer ISLE ROYALE on July 26, 1885, just two miles off her island namesake, is one of those strange coincidences that sometimes occur.

The exact circumstances of the loss are vague, but it seems that she was downbound from Port Arthur to Duluth when she opened her seams in a moderate sea and sank. There was no loss of life, the crew escaping in the gig. Two locations for the loss are given: two miles off Washington Harbor and off Susie Island.

The ISLE ROYALE was originally built in Port Huron as the barge AGNES in 1879. Almost immediately she was sold to a Marine City concern, had an engine and cabins installed and was used as an excursion vessel on the St. Clair River. In 1884 she was sold to the Duluth and North Shore Line and brought up to Lake Superior.

The 91 foot, 55 ton steamer was owned by the Duluth and North Shore Line and used to run passengers and freight between Port Arthur, Isle Royale and Duluth.

BIBLIOGRAPHY

Mansfield, John B. "HISTORY OF THE GREAT LAKES, VOL. 1." Chicago: S.H. Beers, 1899.
"LAKE SUPERIOR NEWS" (Marquette). May 10, 1884.
"MARQUETTE MINING JOURNAL." July 29, 1885.
VanderLinden, Rev. Peter. "GREAT LAKES SHIPS WE REMEMBER." Cleveland: Freshwater Press, 1979.
Wells, Homer C. "History of Accidents and Wrecks on Lake Superior," U.S. Army Corps of Engineers, 1938. Typewritten manuscript in District Engineers Office.

A DAY OF GLORY, A DAY OF LOSS

The morning of November 7, 1885 dawned bright and prosperous for the Canadian Pacific Railroad. Years of labor were being rewarded by the completion of its first trans-Canada rail link. Further south, on the rugged shores of Isle Royale, another drama was being enacted. The CPR steamer ALGOMA, with forty-five passengers and crew, was being destroyed by a vicious Lake Superior gale.

Launched on July 31, 1883, the ALGOMA was a product of the Aitken and Mansell shipyard, Kelvinhaugh, at Whiteinch on the shores of Scotland's Clyde River. Built especially for the CPR, she was 1,773 gross tons, 262 feet in length, 38 feet in beam and 23 feet in depth. Her design

The CPR steamer ALGOMA. One of three sisters, she was thought by many to be unsinkable.

Canadian Pacific Railroad

was to be well proven, evidenced by the long lives of her sisters, the ALBERTA and ATHABASCA, also part of the CPR fleet. Both were finally scrapped in 1948, after 65 years of use!

The three were built at Scotland because of political considerations. At the time, Canada had no shipyards capable of building steel vessels and it was considered unthinkable for the Canadians to have them built in the United States. The only other solution was Scotland. Scottish built vessels had been famous for many years and the prestige of having them in the line would be excellent.

The ALGOMA had accommodations for 130 first-class passengers and 200 in steerage. She was regarded as virtually unsinkable because of her watertight compartments and was valued at over $300,000.

The ALGOMA's first trip was the trans-Atlantic crossing from her Scottish yard to the mouth of the St. Lawrence River. As with most ships being delivered, she didn't travel empty, but carried a profitable cargo of coal. For the first time and last time the ALGOMA's bow tasted saltwater and met the long Atlantic swells. In all respects, she behaved as the champion she was. At Montreal, she was neatly cut in two and, thus disfigured, was towed through the short St. Lawrence canals, Lake Ontario, and the Welland Canal to Buffalo. There, after reassembly, she continued her journey to Owen Sound and her new owners.

The steamer began her Lake career in May, 1884, carrying immigrants and CPR supplies from Owen Sound to Port Arthur.

Although built from a proven design, the ALGOMA did carry one novel innovation, a Plimsoll Mark. The Plimsoll Mark is painted on the side of a vessel to indicate how heavily (and hence safely) loaded a ship is. The ALGOMA may have been the first vessel on the Great Lakes to be marked so.

The sleek hulled steamer also carried fore and mizzen masts so a press of canvas could be used to supplement the power of her mighty Scottish steam engines.

19

The steamer ALBERTA, the ALGOMA's sistership in the Soo Canal. Note the open bridge wings and furled sails.

Marquette County Historical Society

The ALGOMA, ATHABASCA and ALBERTA were an integral part of the Canadian Pacific Railroad system. They provided a vital link between the Owen Sound Railroad and the one at Port Arthur. As grain was a major item hauled by the CPR, the three sisters often carried grain cargos from the elevators at Port Arthur to the CPR elevators at Owen Sound.

The ALGOMA once had a brush with disaster early in her career. On May 25, 1885, downbound from Port Arthur, she stranded ¾ of a mile west of the Two Hearted River Life Saving Station in eastern Lake Superior. The Life Savers made eight trips out to the steamer in their surfboat, but she was later released without damage.

The ALGOMA traveled almost empty on her final voyage, carrying only five passengers in first class, six in steerage and 540 tons of cargo consisting of 200 tons of railroad steel, 100 tons of copper and 240 tons of general merchandise.

At 4 p.m., November 5, she cast off from the Owen Sound wharf, her huge 1,225 horsepower engine wheezing steam, and steadied on course for the Soo. She passed through the locks without incident the next day and reached Whitefish Bay about 12:00. There she raised her sails, stoked her boiler fires higher and raced along at 15 knots. Port Arthur lay dead ahead and Captain John Moore intended to lose no time in completing his trip.

Late on the night of November 6, Lake Superior spawned one of the ferocious fall gales for which it is notorious. The wind shrieked through the rigging and sails strained with added pressure. Blowing snow obscured vision and combined with flying spray from the rising waves to freeze the rigging and make the decks like a sheet of glass.

By morning of the 7th, the gale had increased its tempo. Freezing rain had begun to fall and the northeast wind was piling the waves higher. The ALGOMA had become a ship possessed. Pushed by her engines and pulled by frozen sails, she pranced through the waves with abandon. To continue was insanity!

Wreckers working over the ALGOMA wreck in June of 1886. A "hard hat" diver's ladder is visible from the barge.

Rutherford B. Hayes Library

Captain Moore ordered the frozen sails lowered. Struggling with frozen lines on an icy deck swept by freezing seas, the crew succeeded. Moore altered his course to the southwest, easing the strain while the sails were lowered. The chore completed, he turned back to the northwest.

Moore now knew that he was dangerously close to the rocky coast of Isle Royale. His normal course probably would have carried him past Rock Harbor, Isle Royale, and a swing to port would move him past Passage Island, into Thunder Bay and home to Port Arthur. His problem was compounded by uncertainty regarding his position. With near-zero visibility and a strong northeast wind on his beam, he could have drifted well south of his intended course, heading directly into Isle Royale.

Believing discretion the better part of valor, Moore decided he would turn and head for the safety of the open lake rather than attempting to navigate the treacherous Isle Royale coast. Shortly after 4:00, the ALGOMA's bow began to swing slowly to starboard, away from Isle Royale and into the open lake. Most of the passengers and crew were tucked away in their bunks, weathering the gale the easy way.

With a shudder, the ALGOMA's swinging stern ran hard upon one of Isle Royale's many underwater sentinels. Seas began sweeping the impaled steamer in quick succession. Flooding was reported in the engine room and after holds. The forward half of the steamer still floated free, rising to meet each incoming wave and placing a terrible strain on the stern, still fast on the rock.

The pre-dawn darkness was broken only by white flashes of waves breaking over the doomed ship. Captain Moore huddled many of the survivors in the stern, where he led them in prayer. Lifeboats were splintered, woodwork snapped and hatch covers were blown off. Waves hammered the stranded steamer like piledrivers. The sound of howling wind and crashing seas was pierced only by the screams of passengers or crewmen swept overboard by the grasping water.

Covered with a heavy coat of winter ice, the ALGOMA is pictured as she docked in Port Arthur (todays Thunder Bay) on November 24, 1884. The steamer ISLE ROYALE is at the right.

University of Detroit

At approximately 6:00, a tearing of metal was heard above the storm. The bow broke free and slipped beneath the waves, carrying away many of the crew and passengers trapped inside.

As the black night finally gave way to dawn, the survivors, still clinging to the stern, saw that they were separated from land by only 70 feet of water.

With courage born of desperation, several crewmen attempted to reach shore in the last lifeboat, so far spared by the waves. Though the lifeboat capsized, some of the crewmen did reach shore, others didn't. The overturned lifeboat and bodies were added to the cauldron of boiling wreckage. Masts, spars, lines, linerings and timber beams floated together—morsels in Davey Jone's stew.

The crewmen, now ashore, could do nothing to assist those still aboard the ALGOMA. All through the day of the 7th, the storm raged, although decreasing in ferocity and eventually dying during the night. On the following day, those ashore made contact with the only inhabitants

The saloon of the ATHABASCA, the ALGOMA's sistership. Notice the splendor of this fine steamer.

McCord Museum of McGill University

The ATHABASCA's dining saloon. The ALGOMA's was identical.

McCord Museum of McGill University

of Isle Royale, a group of fishermen. The fishermen rendered what aid they could and dispatched a boat to Port Arthur for assistance. A raft was constructed by those aboard the ALGOMA and it reached shore after some anxious moments.

Warmed by bonfires, the cold and hungry survivors waited for aid. On Monday, November 9, it came in the form of the steamer ATHABASCA. She had sighted the stern of the ALGOMA while proceeding through the Passage Island Channel. Her boats rescued 14 survivors of Lake Superior's greatest maritime disaster, in terms of lives lost. It is interesting to note that the ALGOMA's other sister, the ALBERTA, outbound from Port Arthur, passed seaward of the ALGOMA at approximately the same time the ALGOMA struck the island. Low visibility had prevented the ALBERTA from witnessing her sister's death.

A Canadian Government investigation found Captain Moore guilty of being far off course and suspended his license for nine months. Although he sailed again as a master, he never again held steady command.

The ALGOMA had hit the southeast side of Mott Island, Isle Royale, two miles northeast of the old Rock Harbor Lighthouse. In the spring and summer of 1886, hard hat salvage divers recovered the boilers, main engine and thirteen smaller engines from the stern which had been swept off its rock perch by winter storms. Also recovered was 200 tons of miscellaneous scrap. The salvaged machinery was used in the CPR steamer MANITOBA, built in 1889 by the Polson Iron Works in Owen Sound to replace the ALGOMA.

The MANITOBA continued in operation until 1950 and was finally scrapped in 1951. All the while, she ran on the ALGOMA's old engine!

In 1903, another salvage firm recovered much of the ALGOMA's steel and copper cargo, as did a second firm in 1905. Exactly how much is open to speculation. Some books specializing in "treasure"ships still list the ALGOMA as containing her full cargo and even add $16,000 in specie as a "sweetener."

The end of a short career. The ALGOMA's stern high on the reef off Mott Island. Note the figures on the rocks at the right.

Canadian Pacific Railroad

The 1886 salvage operation resulted in the addition of another wreck to Lake Superior's long list. The tug GEORGE HAND was blown up in shoal water and wrecked. The crew was unhurt and her machinery was later salvaged. In 1887, the tug CHALLENGE was back at the wreck site and recovered additional machinery and cargo.

In August, 1886, some rather disturbing stories filtered from the island. The tales charged some Isle Royale fishermen with having rifled the bodies of the ALGOMA victims for valuables and sinking the remains in deep water offshore.

The promulgators of these reports were evidently the wreckers who worked over the ALGOMA, salvaging her machinery. They reported finding only two bodies, both pinned in the framework of the wreck. Personal articles of value were found in the fishermen's cabins, but whether they were taken from the bodies or simply washed up on the beach was never determined. The Revenue Cutter

ANDY JOHNSON visited the island and made inquiries concerning the affair, but evidently could not ascertain the truth.

The wreckage field of the ALGOMA starts several yards from the rocky beach in 10 to 15 feet of water, continuing into depths in excess of 150 feet. The field is a jungle of twisted steel hull plates and beams. Pieces of the steamer are heaped on top of one another in a bizarre pattern. It is not unusual to find brass portholes torn in half as if by the hands of a raging giant. Nearly all of the steel sections are covered with a brownish, algae-like growth, giving them an unearthly appearance. Portions of the bottom are littered with pieces of broken china, smashed by the hell of the gale. It is difficult to imagine these twisted, battered remains as once comprising the ALGOMA, pride of the Canadian Pacific Railroad Fleet.

BIBLIOGRAPHY

"ASHLAND PRESS." November 14, 1885.

Barry, James P. "SHIPS OF THE GREAT LAKES." Berkley: Howell-North Books, 1970.

Bowen, Dana Thomas. "SHIPWRECKS OF THE LAKES." Cleveland: Freshwater Press, 1971.

Brown, W. Russell. "Ships at Port Arthur and Fort William," "INLAND SEAS," October, 1945.

Carus, Captain Edward. "100 Years of Disasters on the Great Lakes," unpublished manuscript, 1931.

Correspondence from Canadian Pacific Railway, August 10, 1973.

Correspondence from National Maritime Museum, Greenwich, England, August 31, 1976.

"DAILY TIMES-JOURNAL" (Fort William, Ontario). September 22, 1933.

Dominion of Canada, Department of Marine. "Casualties to Vessels Resulting in Total Loss on the Great Lakes—from 1870 to date," 1975.

"DULUTH TRIBUNE." November 13, 1885.

Frimodig, Mac. "SHIPWRECKS OFF KEWEENAW." Fort Wilkins Natural History Association.

Gillham, Skip. "Memories of the CPR Ships," "TELESCOPE," March - April 1979.

Innis, Harold A. "A HISTORY OF THE CANADIAN PACIFIC RAILWAY." Toronto: University of Toronto, 1971.

Landon, Fred. *"Engines Salvaged from Lake Depths Powered the Manitoba," "INLAND SEAS," winter, 1970.*

Mills, John M. *"CANADIAN COASTAL AND INLAND STEAM VESSELS, 1809 - 1930."* Providence, Rhode Island: Steamship Historical Society of America, 1979.

"MINING JOURNAL" (Marquette, Michigan). November 14, 1885; April 24, May 24, July 10, August 7, 14, 21, 28, 1886; July 23, August 27, 1887.

Register of Wreck Reports, U.S. Life-Saving Service, 1885.

Rieseberg, Harry E. *"FELLS COMPLETE GUIDE TO BURIED TREASURE, LAND AND SEA."* New York: Frederick Fell, 1972.

Roland, Walpole. *"ALGOMA WEST."* Warwick & Sons: Toronto, 1887.

Runge Collection, Milwaukee Public Library.

VanderLinden, Rev. Peter J. ed. *"GREAT LAKES SHIPS WE REMEMBER."* Freshwater Press: Cleveland, 1979.

Welnetz, Bob. *"SHIPS OF THE GREAT LAKES ON POST CARDS, VOLUME TWO."* Manitowoc, Wisconsin: Manitowoc Maritime Museum, 1977.

Williams. W. R. *"Shipwrecks at Isle Royale," INLAND SEAS,"* winter, 1956.

Wolff, Julius F. Jr. *"Canadian Shipwrecks on Lake Superior," "INLAND SEAS,"* spring, 1978.

WRECKING THE WRECKER

In order to minimize their losses in the ALGOMA disaster, the CPR contracted an Algonac, Michigan wrecking firm to salvage the steamers machinery. To accomplish the task, the firm dispatched the tug GEORGE HAND with the schooner L.L. LAMB to work the wreck. Throughout the summer of 1886, the wreckers worked away, salvaging the remains of the once proud steamer.

But on August 9, disaster struck. A sudden squall blew the GEORGE HAND on the rocks about 500 yards from Little Schooner Island. Resting on her starboard side in about four feet of water, she was a shambles. Luckily, no lives were lost.

Undaunted by the unexpected turn of events, the wreckers soon went to work on the tug, salvaging whatever they could. Additional work on the tug was also accomplished in 1887.

BIBLIOGRAPHY

"FREE PRESS" (Detroit). August 12, 13, 14, 15, 18, 20, 21, 26, 1886.
"JOURNAL OF THE LIGHT-STATION OF MENAGERIE ISLAND." June - August, 1886. National Archives and Records Service. Washington, D.C.
"MINING JOURNAL" (Marquette, Michigan). August 14, 21, 28, 1886.

A.B. TAYLOR

Another minor Isle Royale stranding occurred on July 23, 1890 when the small 106 foot steamer A.B. TAYLOR became disoriented in a fog and ran hard on a reef about a mile and a half southwest of Menagerie Island.

Later that day the lighthouse tender WARRINGTON tried to pull her free but was unsuccessful and left. The following day the Booth Line steamer HIRAM R. DIXON, while on her regular run, sighted the TAYLOR and after some heavy pulling, tugged the stubborn vessel free. The TAYLOR continued on her trip apparently having suffered no major damages.

The TAYLOR was built in 1884 at Saugatuck, Michigan by R.C. Brittain. 94 gross tons, she was 106 feet in length, 20 feet in beam and 7.8 feet in depth. In 1902 she

The A.B. TAYLOR, shown here as the OTTAWA.

was sold, rebuilt and renamed OTTAWA. She ended her days on December 14, 1910 when she burned at Cape Vincent, New York, while owned by the Thousand Island Steamboat Company.

BIBLIOGRAPHY

"FREE PRESS" (Detroit). July 25, 1890.
"LOG OF THE LIGHT-STATION AT MENAGERIE ISLAND, OCTO-BER - NOVEMBER, 1890." National Archives, Washington, D.C.
"UNIVERSITY OF DETROIT, MARINE HISTORICAL COLLECTION."
Van der Linden, Rev. Peter, ed. "GREAT LAKES SHIPS WE REMEM-BER." Cleveland: Freshwater Press. 1979.

DUMP IT OVERBOARD. . .
THE CENTURION'S STRANDED

Again and again the rolling seas of the northwest gale slammed into the CENTURION's blunt steel bow. Each wave sent a shower of cold water high over the pilothouse. Inside, the captain looked out into the storm, searching anxiously for some glimpse of Isle Royale. He knew the island was just ahead of him, but low-scudding clouds and intermittent snow squalls made for poor visibility. Nearly blinded by the elements, he continued to grope forward.

It was Monday, October 28, 1895. On Saturday, the 26th, the CENTURION had departed Superior, Wisconsin, downbound with 27,000 barrels of flour and feed and 600 tons of Montana copper ingots. Caught by the gale, her captain elected to run to the shelter of Isle Royale's Siskiwit Bay rather than face the storm on the wild stretches of the open lake. Unknown to the captain, another demon lay ahead. It would grab and hold his vessel in its rocky fist.

Because of poor visibility, the captain was obviously confused with respects to his true position. At 5:00 a.m., Monday, the CENTURION drove hard and fast on a reef which guards the entrance to Siskiwit Bay. The CENTURION's steel hull had bumped and scraped its way over the reef until she rested amidships and was more than 20 inches up in the water. Luckily, the steamer had been constructed with a double bottom and the inner hull was not heavily damaged. She maintained her watertight integrity, remaining, nevertheless, firmly wedged on the reef.

Although the CENTURION was sheltered from the

northwest gale, any shift of the seas to the northeast or southwest would likely destroy her. Immediate action was required if the CENTURION was to be saved. The steamer and her cargo were valued at $400,000, not a sum to be surrendered without a struggle.

Doing the only thing he could to save his vessel, the captain reluctantly ordered the cargo thrown overboard, beginning with the heavy copper ingots. He could hopefully reduce the CENTURION's draft enough to allow her powerful engine to pull her free.

The crew worked desperately at their task. No time could be lost if the vessel was to be saved. They could not sit idly by waiting for a salvage tug. They had to act!

On Tuesday, the small Booth Line steamer HIRAM R. DIXON, a forerunner of the AMERICA, sighted the CENTURION, but the sea was still heavy and she was unable to approach alongside. The DIXON did, however, carry the news of the wreck to Duluth.

The Duluth wrecking firm of B.B. Inman and Company dispatched their tug from Duluth and wired Marquette for the tug CASTLE with its wrecking gear. They were to rendezvous at the site. The CASTLE had been standing by in Marquette, waiting to free the schooner-barges MOONLIGHT and KENT from the beach where a September gale had stranded them.

Sometime after the DIXON departed the CENTURION, the brand new, 351-foot steamer PENOBSCOT arrived. In a feat of fine seamanship, her master was able to maneuver close enough to offload part of the CENTURION's flour and some of the copper. As most of the copper had already been dumped, the crew (with some Isle Royale fishermen giving a hand) had already begun jettisoning the flour. The PENOBSCOT then put a line aboard the CENTURION and worked for 12 hours in an effort to pull the steamer off.

At 7:00 p.m., October 30, she succeeded and the CENTURION floated free. The inner hull of the steamer continued to hold and no difficulty was encountered in keeping her afloat despite a leak which had developed forward of the collision bulkhead.

The Inman tugs arrived, sighting the CENTURION free of the reef, under her own power and enroute to Duluth. They followed, ready to assist. The CENTURION reached Duluth at 9:00 a.m., Thursday and immediately began to offload her remaining cargo.

The Inman Company was given the contract to recover the dumped copper at a rate of 10% of value. The W.H. Singer Company was engaged to salvage what it could of the estimated 1,000 barrels of jettisoned flour at a rate of 50% of value.

Inman worked at the copper recovery project throughout the fall, battling gales and storms that frequently drove the salvors off the CENTURION reef. The water wasn't deep, from 13 to 30 feet, but the bottom was jagged. The hard hat divers were forced to grope carefully between the rocks and into deep crevices in search of the elusive copper ingots. It was a difficult task for divers equipped with bulky hard hat outfits. Each bar had to be secured to a lifting cable and hoisted to the surface with a derick and donkey steam engine. It was grueling work.

The salvors fought not only the weather and the difficult bottom, but the pillaging efforts of other would-be salvors. Notable are the exploits of Captain Martin Daniels of Marquette and the schooner CHRIS GROVER. Captain Daniels was a sailor in the best tradition—he possessed the soul of a Blackbeard and the skill of a Drake!

Daniels' exploits in the Marquette area were legendary and his salt water sailing days had seen him wrecked eight times. In 1880, he lost his schooner TOM BOY in a gale off Marquette and brought his total to nine. In any event, Daniels arrived safely at the wreck site and began to salvage any of the flour he could locate.

After a week, Daniels had recovered some 7,000 pounds in fair condition. At one point he was apparently confronted by a representative of the Singer Company demanding that he turn over his cargo. Daniels' response will never be known, but we trust that he carefully explained the purpose and function of a capstan bar while reflecting on the Singer representative's ancestry. . .

Daniels did nearly increase his shipwreck experiences to 10 during the course of the unauthorized salvage operations when heavy weather almost blew him on the rocks of Passage Island. In a desperate effort, he let go his anchor with 100 fathoms of cable bent on for good measure. The anchor caught and held, saving the CHRIS GROVER from certain destruction. When Daniels attempted to leave, however, he discovered that the anchor had been hopelessly fouled and he was forced to leave it and the cable.

Much of the flour (in sacks) was also recovered by Isle Royale fishermen. It provided a welcome addition to their meager fare for years to come. The use of such shipwrecked flour had occurred before, most notable when the steamer MANISTEE went missing in November, 1883. Barreled flour from her had washed ashore along the western beaches of the Keweenaw Peninsula and was eagerly sought by area residents. The outer part of the flour had become wet, but that had solidified and formed a seal. The inner portion remained quite dry and useable.

Although the CENTURION reached Duluth safely, her troubles were far from over.

First, the PENOBSCOT libled her and her remaining cargo for $20,000, claiming the amount was owed for releasing the CENTURION from the reef and stating that the work was done at great danger to herself. It undoubtedly was.

The CENTURION eventually posted $40,000 in bonds to cover the salvage claim.

Then there were delays in drydocking. Other vessels were there before her and their repairs took longer than expected.

When the water in the West Superior drydock finally drained away, the CENTURION's wounds were bared for all to see. Part of the outer steel hull had been stoved in as much as two feet and 60 hull plates were so badly damaged that replacement was required. Over ¾ of her hull length had received some form of damage. The battered steamer spent more than three weeks in dry-dock and as many as 275 yard workers were involved in her repair. The costs eventually topped $20,000, but by December 5 she was out of the dock and back in service, taking a cargo of grain from Fort William to Buffalo. It was her last trip of the year.

By the end of the 1895 season, the Inman salvors had recovered 200 tons of copper. The bulk of the remainder was picked up the following year. The tantalizing possibility exists, though, that some of it is still on the reef.

The CENTURION was a fairly new vessel, built in 1893 as hull number 100 in the Bay City yard of the F.W. Wheeler Company. She was 360 feet in length, 45 feet in beam and 3,401 gross tons. Owned by the Hopkins Transportation Company, she sailed under charter to the Anchor Line. The CENTURION had a long and useful life, eventually being scrapped in 1945 as the ALEX B. URIG.

Two of the main actors in the CENTURION episode, the PENOBSCOT and the CHRIS GROVER, both later became Lake Superior shipwrecks themselves. In August of 1899, the PENOBSCOT had her compass stray due to a magnetic fluxuation and ran onto the beach near Knife Island, northeast of Duluth. Although she was later released, damages were extensive. The CHRIS GROVER was driven on a reef near Split Rock, Minnesota during an October, 1899 gale and destroyed.

BIBLIOGRAPHY

Bowen, Dana Thomas. "MEMORIES OF THE LAKES." Cleveland: Freshwater Press, 1969.

"DAILY MINING JOURNAL" (Marquette), November 2, 7, 1895.

"FREE PRESS" (Detroit). October 30, 31; November 1, 2, 6, 9, 10, 22, 30; December 5, 7, 9, 1895.

Holden, Thomas R., "Park Interpretation as an Environmental Communication Process With a Sample Interpretive Booklet Text on the Maritime Disaster of Siskiwit Bay, Isle Royale, Lake Superior." Unpublished Master's Thesis, University of Wisconsin - Madison, 1974.

Mason, George C. "A List of The Hulls Built by F.W. Wheeler and Company," "INLAND SEAS," October, 1945.

"MERCHANT VESSELS OF THE UNITED STATES," various years.

Stonehouse, Frederick, "MARQUETTE SHIPWRECKS." Marquette Harboridge Press, 1974.

Wolff, Julius F., "LAKE SUPERIOR SHIPWRECKS OF THE 1890's." Social Sciences Research Trust Fund Publication Number 6. University of Minnesota, 1961.

Wolff, Julius F., "THE SHIPWRECKS OF LAKE SUPERIOR." Duluth: Lake Superior Marine Museum Association, 1979.

Wright, Richard J., "FRESHWATER WHALES." Kent, Ohio: Kent State University Press, 1969.

HENRY CHISHOLM

On Sunday evening, October 16, 1898, the 256-foot wooden steamer HENRY CHISHOLM loaded a cargo of 92,000 bushels of barley and departed Duluth, downbound for the Soo and ports below. Following at the end of a towline was the 220-foot schooner-barge JOHN MARTIN. The MARTIN's hold and decks were piled high with 1,200,000 feet of lumber. Both vessels were owned by M.A. Bradley of Cleveland.

At the turn of the century, schooner-barges like the JOHN MARTIN were very common on the Great Lakes. Such vessels were originally built as schooners, but when steam took over as the primary motive power, they had their sail rig shortened and assumed the role of barges. In a pinch they could sail, although not very well.

The two vessels proceeded until Monday evening when they reached a point off the Keweenaw Peninsula's northern tip and ran smack into a gale. The MARTIN's towline, strained by the increasing violence of the storm, parted.[1] The schooner immediately set her fore and mainsails and was soon lost to view in the heavy weather.

When the weather let up, the CHISHOLM began a search for the missing MARTIN. By Thursday morning, her unsuccessful efforts had taken her to the south end of Isle Royale. At 8 a.m., in an attempt to enter Washington Harbor, the CHISHOLM ran hard up on the unmarked Rock of Ages Reef.[2] The force of the collisiion was so great that the steamer was driven out more than two feet forward, and her hull was so badly shattered that water flooded to her lower deck. The CHISHOLM's position was dangerous. The reef was open to seas from every direction. It was no place for a ship's crew to be, and

Captain Smith and his 15-man crew knew it! They abandoned her and rowed to Isle Royale, three miles away.

With the crew safe ashore, Smith ordered his Mate, Mr. Wilesman, and five crewmen to row to Port Arthur in the yawl and report the steamer's predicament. As luck would have it, the steamer HIRAM DIXON sighted the yawl offshore and picked up its occupants. The DIXON's skipper delivered them to Port Arthur to make their report.

On Friday, a B.B. Inman tug arrived at the wreck and attempted to drain her with two pumps. But the salvors were unable to lower the water an inch. The hull of the steamer was too badly punctured by the rocks. As quickly as the water was expelled, more water rushed in.

The CHISHOLM's crew was plucked off the Island and sent down lake on the steamer CITY OF CLEVE-LAND, also owned by M.A. Bradley.

Meanwhile, the MARTIN turned up safe and sound at the Soo on Friday evening. It isn't clear whether she sailed the entire distance or was picked up off Copper Harbor and towed by the steamer ROMAN. To sail the entire distance with her shortened rig would have been difficult, so she probably had a tow.

On Wednesday, October 26, a northwest gale spelled the end of the steamer HENRY CHISHOLM. Battered by the Superior norther', she slipped off the reef and sank in deep water. Two years later, the MARTIN also became a Great Lakes shipwreck, sinking off Port Huron with a loss of four hands.

The CHISHOLM wreck is in approximately 150 feet of water just a short distance from the GEORGE M. COX. Much of the wreckage is superimposed on the wreck of the CUMBERLAND, lost on the reef in 1877.

In 1901, wreckers recovered both of the CHISHOLM's boilers, but apparently due to its age, left the engine. The massive engine, with 30 and 56 inch diameter cylinders and a 48 inch stroke, was built by the Globe Iron Works in 1880. Sitting upright, it presents a spectacular visual image to the diver.

HENRY CHISHOLM

1880 - Oct. 16, 1898
Length   256'
Beam   39'
Depth   20'

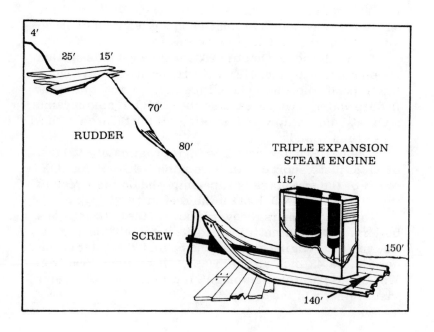

4'

25'   15'

70'

RUDDER

80'

TRIPLE EXPANSION
STEAM ENGINE

115'

SCREW

150'

140'

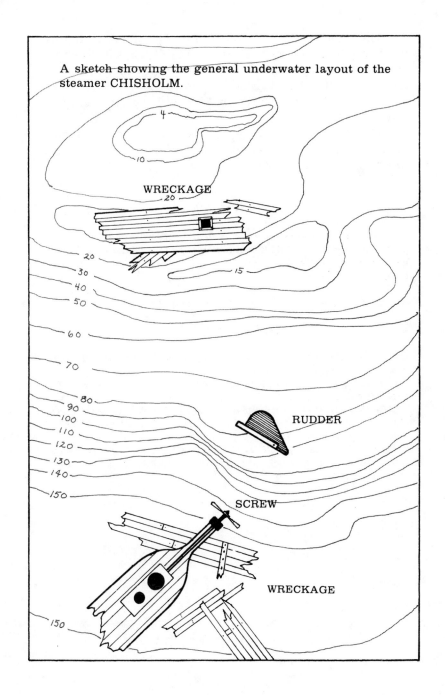

A sketch showing the general underwater layout of the steamer CHISHOLM.

WRECKAGE

RUDDER

SCREW

WRECKAGE

The HENRY CHISHOLM, Official number 95610, was built in Cleveland in 1880 at a cost of $125,000. Technically a wooden propeller, she was 1,775 gross tons, 256.5 feet in length, 39 feet in beam and 20 feet in depth. The JOHN MARTIN was built in 1873 and registered at 937 tons.

The CHISHOLM was valued at $70,000 and her grain cargo at $42,000. The vessel was unfortunately, but not untypically, *not* insured.

FOOTNOTES

1. *Accounts of this are somewhat unclear. It isn't beyond the realm of possibility that the MARTIN cut her towline to ease the strain of the gale. With a short sail rig set she could have ridden the gale out in comparative safety.*

2. *The present day lighthouse wasn't erected until 1908.*

BIBLIOGRAPHY

Carus, Captain Edward. *"100 Years of Disasters on the Great Lakes,"* unpublished manuscript, 1931.
Consolidated Certificate of Enrollment and License, Steamer HENRY CHISHOLM, 1880, 1895.
"FREE PRESS" (Detroit). October 22, 23, 25, 27, 1898, October 23, 1900.
Holden, Thom. *"Reef of the Three C's: Part II," "THE NOR'EASTER,"* March - April, 1978.
"MERCHANT VESSELS OF THE UNITED STATES," various issues.
Williams W.R. *"Shipwrecks at Isle Royale," "INLAND SEAS,"* winter 1956, p. 252

THE 'HARLEM' OF HARLEM REEF

On November 26, 1898, a month and six days after the HENRY CHISHOLM ran up on Rock of Ages Reef, another vessel met one of Isle Royale's dangerous shoals. For the CHISHOLM, the meeting had become a life-long relationship. It threatened to become one for the HARLEM.

The steel steamer HARLEM was built in 1888 as hull number 84 at the Wyandotte, Michigan yard of the Detroit Drydock Company. Registered at 2,299 gross tons, she was 288 feet in length, 41 feet in beam and 23 feet in depth. Her 1,700 hp, triple expansion engine was built as number 147 by the Drydock Engine Works in 1888. The HARLEM and her sister ship, the HUDSON, were owned by the New York Central Railroad (Western Transit Company) and were named for New York's famous Harlem and Hudson Rivers. Both vessels were known as fast boats and excellent money earners.[1]

The HARLEM was upbound for Duluth when the stranding occurred. There were really no special circumstances leading up to the accident. It was just a repeat of what happened many times before to other vessels and it would happen many times after.

Upon clearing the Soo Canal the HARLEM ran headlong into a classic Superior norther'. The HARLEM was big enough and staunch enough to take that kind of heavy weather so she pushed on, shoving aside the cresting waves and forcing her way slowly toward Duluth.

Then Superior threw HARLEM a curve. The gale cranked up and began to test the steamer. Twelve-foot waves grew to 15-footers, and then mounted to 20 feet. The wind began to scream. Clearly, the HARLEM was going to find the going extremely difficult.

The HARLEM shortly after coming off her Isle Royale perch. Notice the stern of one tug behind her port bow and another off her stern.

Lake Superior Marine Museum

But her captain was no fool. He headed his charge for the shelter of Isle Royale's east coast. Once he got within several miles of shore, the force of the gale would be broken by the island's mass. He could then run along the coast—south to Duluth. It was a good plan, but not good enough.

The gale had already reduced visibility and the captain could not "pick up" the coast of Isle Royale.[2] When he finally did sight the island, it was too late. The HARLEM was up on a shoal just south of the reef CENTURION had hit three years before. The shoal is now known as Harlem Reef and is 4 ¾ miles south of Menagerie Island.

Luckily, the HARLEM had run hard enough on the reef to prevent her from slipping off. As long as the gale kept to the north and west, the steamer and her crew were relatively safe. But if it shifted to the south or east their position would become precarious.

The news of the steamer's predicament first reached Duluth on November 18, via the steamer THOMPSON which had sighted her the day before. Two tugs, each outfitted with diver and heavy pumps, were dispatched to her aid, but the wreckers couldn't float the steamer free.

When the MILWAUKEE, another Western Transit Company steamer, enroute from Duluth to Buffalo, stopped by her stricken sister on December 1, she learned that the HARLEM was in bad shape. The HARLEM's mate took the chance to row out to the MILWAUKEE in the yawl and report the situation. The HARLEM was filled with water to her main deck and had begun to break in two, forward of the boiler room. The bow was down to the 10-foot mark and the stern was sunk below the main deck. The crew had abandoned her and was living at the Menagerie Island Light. There was still an opportunity, however, to salvage some of the cargo.

Additional reports reaching Duluth concerning the steamer's condition were, at best, confused. Some indi-

The HARLEM drydocked after her Isle Royale excursion.

Lake Superior Marine Museum

45

cated that she would be refloated soon. Others had the HARLEM a total loss with salvage only a forlorn hope. Perhaps the most pessimistic report had a hard-hat diver working on her, entering the water over her side and surfacing through a hole in her bottom!

Ignoring public opinion, the salvors continued to work on the wreck. Patching and pumping, they did their best to haul the HARLEM off her perch. By mid- December, the wreckers gave up. If she was still there in the spring they would try again.

Their efforts did result in 300 of the 1,180 tons of her sugar, salt and cement cargo being salvaged. The value of the total cargo was estimated at $50,000. The steamer itself was priced at $225,000.

When the salvors returned in the spring, the HARLEM was still on the reef! Winter gales had pivoted her a bit, but she still looked "reasonably good." There was new damage, however. The mizzen mast had snapped off three feet above the deck and she had buckled some amidships.

The Western Transit Company meanwhile had collected on the insurance from the underwriters who, in turn, were very interested in the value of their new possession, the hopeless HARLEM.

Having no other choice, they advertised her for sale. After representatives of the various Great Lakes salvage companies inspected her in May, a high bid was accepted from the Thompson Towing and Wrecking Company of Port Huron for $30,000. This was rather surprising because the Thompson Company was virtually unknown. Experts didn't think the company's chances for success were very good. Nevertheless, on June 10, 1899, under the direction of Captain Washington Harrow, salvage work had begun.

On August 20 they succeeded in pulling a reluctant HARLEM off her reef. Her cargo actually helped save her. The packaged cement had mixed with the water, and though it clogged the pumps, it also plugged many of the small leaks in the hull. The HARLEM repaired herself!

But the cement posed some problems too. Before the salvors could move the HARLEM to a sheltering bay, the pumps clogged on the cement and only good fortune enabled the steamer to be hauled onto a nearby reef where she was allowed to settle.

Again, the weary salvors began to work at the reluctant steamer. The HARLEM had become a challenge. She had assumed a life of her own and they were damned if they would let her beat them. They patched and pumped and unclogged pumps and shored up weakened bulkheads. It was a battle of epic proportions and they would win it, or die trying!

The HARLEM after her midships deckhouse was moved aft. Both topmasts have been cut down and the center mast removed.

K.E. Thro Collection

On Wednesday, September 27, the HARLEM again was afloat and this time the salvors had her under control. They pulled her carefully into the shelter of Little Siskiwit Bay, where necessary repairs could be made before the long tow to a dry dock.[3]

The salvors worked through early fall to prepare the steamer for the long tow to Port Huron for permanent repairs. Finally, on October 25, the lake was calm. . .and the HARLEM was ready. By 6:00 p.m., the HARLEM, under the tow of the tug W.F. MERRICK, had survived the 60-mile trip to the Keweenaw Waterway and was safe in the Lily Pond. It had been a fast tow, lasting only six hours.

Interest in the steamer ran high in the Copper Country and many local residents took the opportunity to examine the famous wreck. Visitors reported that the salvors had managed the resurrection of the HARLEM's two boilers and were using their power to run the pumps. She was still leaking badly, but the water could be held in check.

On October 28, the HARLEM departed the Waterway under tow and arrived in Port Huron on November 6.

Launched sideways in traditional Great Lakes fashion, the HARLEM slides down the ways at the Wyandotte, Michigan yard of the Detroit Drydock Company.

Mariners Museum

There she was drydocked for a careful survey of damages. It was decided to rebuild her to the original specifications and she was then towed to Toledo where better facilities were available.

The Thompson Company made a handsome profit on their investment. They had gambled $30,000 in purchasing a nearly hopeless wreck and put out another $30,000 in salvage expenses. With the rebuilding costing $75,000, they had invested $135,000 in a vessel valued at $225,000. Their profit of $90,000 was handsome by anyone's standard!

From this point on, the HARLEM led a "checkered" life. She left Toledo rebuilt as a bulk freighter. From then until her eventual abandonment at Jacksonville, Florida, as a floating hotel in 1930, she had ten owners. On September 20, 1902, the HARLEM stranded again, this time running hard on Mouse Island Reef, northwest of Marblehead on Lake Erie. After lightering much cargo, she was pulled free on the 22nd by the tug WALES. Without a shade of doubt, though, the highlight of the vessel's life was when she was the HARLEM of Harlem Reef.

FOOTNOTES

1. *Both vessels were somewhat ill-starred. The HARLEM obviously for her stranding at Isle Royale, and the HUDSON as she would sink in 1901 off Eagle River with all hands.*

2. *Author's note: I've been in a similar position and it's damned frustrating!*

3. *Little Siskiwit Bay is not listed on any contemporary charts or maps.*

BIBLIOGRAPHY

"FREE PRESS" (Detroit). November 29, December 3, 6, 9, 1898; October 4, 21, 26, November 12, 17, 1899.
Holden, Thomas R. "Park Interpretation as an Environmental Communications Process With a Sample Interpretive Booklet Text on the Maritime Disaster History of Siskiwit Bay, Isle Royale, Lake Superior," unpublished master's thesis, University of Wisconsin - Madison, 1974. Lake Superior Marine Museum Collection: Duluth, Minnesota.

Mason, George C. *"A Partial List of Hull Numbers of Ships Built by the Component Shipyards Making up the American Shipbuilding Company, Cleveland, Ohio." "INLAND SEAS," winter, 1952.*

"MERCHANT VESSELS OF THE UNITED STATES," various issues.

"MINING JOURNAL" (Marquette, Michigan). December 10, 1890; September 11, 18, 29, 1899.

University of Detroit, Marine Historical Collection. Detroit, Michigan.

United States Life-Saving Service. "ANNUAL REPORT, 1902." Washington, D.C.: U.S. Government Printing Office, 1903.

Wells, Homer C. *"History of Accidents and Wrecks on Lake Superior."* U.S. Army Corps of Engineers, 1938. Typewritten manuscript in District Engineers Office.

Williams, W.R. *"Shipwrecks at Isle Royale," "INLAND SEAS,"* winter, 1956.

A TALE OF TWO WHALEBACKS

Without doubt, the most unusual class of vessel ever built on the Great Lakes was the Whaleback. From 1888 to 1898, 43 of these strange-looking ships were launched . . .most at the Superior, Wisconsin yard of the American Steel Barge Company.

The whaleback was the inventive creation of Captain Alexander McDougall, a Great Lakes master of rare ability and insight. The theory behind McDougall's design was simple. He reasoned that a hull with a rounded deck and sides would have much less resistance to the wind and waves than a conventional vessel. Since whalebacks had watertight hatches, they could run safely with their decks completely underwater.

It looked for awhile as if Captain McDougall's idea would revolutionize shipbuilding, but the design never quite caught the shipbuilders' fancy. Shipbuilders, like insurance underwriters, are a notoriously staid group.

McDougall's theory, however, was a valid one. The whalebacks proved to be fine vessels, although some difficulty was experienced in heavy weather when they were not fully loaded. The design was eventually abandoned when the demand for larger vessels precluded additional whaleback construction. From an engineering standpoint they could not be built large enough without encountering a host of structural problems.

Some of the whalebacks were built as barges and others as steamers. One, the CHRISTOPHER COLUMBUS, was constructed as a passenger vessel. The 362-foot COLUMBUS was initially used as an excursion steamer for the 1898 Chicago World's Fair. She later ran as a regular passenger steamer and had a long and safe career, finally being withdrawn from service in 1931 and scrapped in 1936. During this 33-year span she carried more passengers than any other vessel on the Great Lakes.

Some whalebacks sailed "foreign." The CHARLES W. WETMORE carried wheat from Duluth across the stormy Atlantic to England and general cargo around the gale-swept horn to Washington. The WETMORE continued her salty career, eventually circumnavigating the globe and becoming the first American steamer to pass through the Suez Canal.

The whaleback SAGAMORE, built in Sunderland, England, in 1893, was used in the Mediterranean and Black Sea grain trade. A World War I torpedo sank her off Spain in 1917.

The whaleback (derisively known as a "pigboat"), was a scrappy vessel. Though many were wrecked, it was never because they were whalebacks; but more that they, like so many vessels, were caught in the claws of fate.

Isle Royale's association with the whalebacks is limited to one rather small area, Rainbow Cove, on the southern end of the island. It was there that two whalebacks, the FRANK ROCKEFELLER and the JOHN B. TREVOR were blown ashore.

The ROCKEFELLER fetched up on November 3, 1905, during a blinding snowstorm. The steamer was laden with 4,900 tons of ore and towing the 375-foot barge MAIDA with an additional 5,700 tons. When the steamer jolted to a halt, the barge, still with a large amount of way on her, crashed heavily into the ROCKEFELLER's stern, badly damaging the rudder.

Captain P.A. Patterson escaped with his crew on a fishing boat to Port Arthur and notified the owners. Immediately salvage operations were started. After a week of hard work by the steamer MARITANA and the tugs FAVORITE, RESCUE and S.C. SCHENCH, the whaleback was released, but only after dumping 1,700 tons of ore. Damages were estimated at $9,000, a slight amount considering the ROCKEFELLER alone was valued at $225,000.

The 2,759-ton ROCKEFELLER was launched as hull number 136 in April, 1896. The steamer was 366 feet long and 45 feet in beam. Later sold and renamed the SOUTH PARK, she carried grain, sand, coal and even automobiles. In 1943 she was sold again, renamed the METEOR and converted to an oil tanker.

As the METEOR, she continued in service until 1969 when she ran aground near Marquette. Although damages were slight, she couldn't pass a Coast Guard inspection without an overhaul. Electing not to invest more money in a 73-year old vessel, the owners decided to donate her to the Head of the Lakes Maritime Society. She is now in Superior, Wisconsin on exhibit as a museum ship.

On October 11, 1909, the second of the Rainbow Cove whalebacks arrived. The JOHN B. TREVOR was upbound for Two Harbors with a cargo of coal when a 60-mph gale forced her onto the beach between the cove and Grace Harbor. For three days she was bounced on the beach, the gale working over the stranded whaleback without respite. The sweeping gray waves forced the steamer 150 feet up the beach from her original landing point!

Word of the wreck was brought to the Soo by the 432-foot steel steamer CURRY.

When the wreckers finally arrived, they found the steamer in sad shape. Pounded by the waves, her bottom was badly damaged and the cargo hold flooded. The engine had been forced up six inches from its mounting and the air pipes were driven 15 inches through the weather deck.

The salvors, led by the veteran wrecking tug FAVORITE, worked over the wreck without success. They pumped, lightered and pulled, but the beached beast wouldn't budge. Even the presence of Captain McDougall couldn't inspire his creation to slide off her new-found home. The owners handed her over to the insurance underwriters. They had better luck.

The TREVOR was hauled off the following year and towed to Port Arthur for repairs. There she waited with the salvaged DUNELM for completion of the new Port Arthur drydock. She and the DUNELM were the first vessels repaired at the facility.

The TREVOR was 308 feet long, 38 feet in beam, 24 feet deep and 1,713 gross tons. She was launched as hull number 135 in 1895. The steamer was later sold Canadian and renamed the ATIKOKAN. In 1922 she was lengthened to 365 feet. A simple change of name didn't prevent another wreck. On August 17, 1913, the ATIKOKAN became disabled on the St. Clair River and ran on the beach at Marine City. She remained in service until 1935 when she was sent to the ship breakers at Halifax.

The whaleback JOHN B. TREVOR alongside an ore dock.

Dossin Great Lakes Institute

The two whalebacks, the John B. TREVOR and the FRANK ROCKEFELLER, were built together in the shipyard and wrecked together at Rainbow Cove.

The FRANK ROCKEFELLER (now METEOR) is a museum ship in Superior, Wisconsin. She is the only surviving example of this unique breed of Great Lakes vessel.

Mariners Museum

STR. ATIKOKEN AT MARINE CITY. 8\17\13.

A.M.M SOL

The whaleback ATIKOKEN ashore at Marine City, Michigan in 1913. As the JOHN B. TREVOR she was ashore at Isle Royale in 1909.

Runge Collection

BIBLIOGRAPHY

Bowen, Dana Thomas. *"MEMORIES OF THE GREAT LAKES."* Cleveland: Freshwater Press, 1969.

Certificate of Enrollment, JOHN B. TREVOR, 1896

"DAILY MINING GAZETTE" (Houghton). October 13, November 17, 1909.

"DAILY MINING JOURNAL" (Marquette). November 13, 1905.

"DAILY TIMES JOURNAL" (Fort William, Ontario). October 18, 1909.

Dowling, Rev. E.J. *"The Tin Stacks, The Story of the Ships of the Pittsburgh Steamship Company."* *"INLAND SEAS",* winter, 1953.

"EVENING TELEGRAM" (Superior, Wisconsin). October 13, 21, 1909.

Lydecker, Ryck. *"PIGBOAT, THE STORY OF THE WHALEBACKS."* Duluth: Sweetwater Press 1973.

"MERCHANT VESSELS OF THE UNITED STATES," various issues.

"PLAIN DEALER" (Cleveland). October 18, 1909.

Sanborn, Janet Coe. *"THE AUTOBIOGRAPHY OF CAPTAIN ALEXANDER McDOUGALL."* Cleveland: Great Lakes Historical Society, 1968.

Wolff, Julius F. *"Shipwrecks of Lake Superior, 1900 - 1909."* *"INLAND SEAS,"* spring, 1972.

AN OLD 'PRIDE OF THE LINE' COMES TO THE END OF THE LINE

The wind came straight out of the north and whistled across the harbor. Where water lay undisturbed, it began to freeze into a thin sheet of ice. Huddled figures hauled the bow spring aboard a steamer and shivered in the cold, their muttered oaths freezing in the air. Great black balls of smoke curled out of a tall dark stack. The S.S. MONARCH slowly eased away from her Port Arthur dock.

The MONARCH in her earlier days.

Runge Collection

It was December 6, 1906, the last trip of the season for the MONARCH and her crew was glad. It had been a long hard year and they were looking forward to spending Christmas with their families.

Her holds were filled with 85,000 bushels of wheat from the great Canadian grain fields, a cargo that would command a fine price of $125,000 when she reached Sarnia. She also held a quantity of canned salmon and barreled flour.

Heavy snow began to fall even before the MONARCH cleared Thunder Bay. It soon worked itself into a full blizzard. Visibility was nil. The blizzard and the seas increased in ferocity until a moderate gale was running. Clear water broke over the ship's wooden bow and swept down her decks, steaming back into the lake.

Under the direction of her master, Captain Edward Robertson, a veteran of 35 years of sailing, the steamer's watch kept a careful lookout. Their eyes continued to search the white gloom despite the blizzard. To check his "dead reckoning," Robertson ordered the engineer to "take the log."

"The log" was a taffrail log, a mechanical device which trailed behind the steamer to record the distance run. It would help give an approximation of their position.

Some of the passengers and crew left their warm cabins and came on deck when they heard the captain's order about the log. Checking the log so early in a trip was unusual. On deck, though, the blizzard prevented their seeing more than a dozen yards, so, with their curiosity satisfied, they went back below.

On the bridge the helmsman suddenly announced that he "thought" he saw Passage Island Light through the snow. But the time was wrong. It was too soon. They should not be seeing it yet. Something was terribly amiss. But if it wasn't the Passage Island Light, what was it?

Shortly after 9:00 p.m. it no longer mattered.

The MONARCH struck hard on the rocks with a splintering crash. Lake water poured into the engine room through seams opened by the impact. Robertson's quick estimation was that their only hope for survival lay in keeping the MONARCH afloat as long as possible. To do that, he would have to keep the battered bow on the rocks so that no more water could enter through the gapping holes.

Quick orders were passed to the engine room, "keep her running!" The boilers remained fired despite rising water and the huge engine was kept running.

Slowly, but with enormous thrust, the MONARCH's great propeller turned, holding the steamer on the rocks. If she slipped off she would quickly slide to an icy grave and take her crew with her.

The first faint streaks of dawn illuminated the towering rock palisades of Blake's Point, Isle Royale. Though their situation was still desperate, the MONARCH's captain and crew at least now knew where they were!

An attempt was made to run a line ashore with a lifeboat. A rock projected only 25 feet away, but the boat couldn't make a landing and was smashed.

An unusual method was used to get a line to the beach. A deckhand, J.D. McCullum, had a rope tied around his waist and was lowered nearly to the surface of the water. Then he was swung pendulum-fashion until he was over the projecting rock. There he was released.

Twice he was thrown to the rock, but each time he slipped off. He was hauled out both times and the process was repeated.

The third time the rope broke, but the deckhand landed on the rock and managed to hold on. A ladder was passed from the ship and he was able to climb to the top of the high cliffs with the running end of a line. After he secured his end to a tree, the crew of the MONARCH drew it taut. Now they could begin to cross to safety.

One at a time the 32 crewmen and 12 passengers dangled out high above the churning lake. All of them survived the dangerous crossing over the freezing water, except for a watchman who, apparently confused, mistakenly slid down a fender line into the boiling lake and his death! In the best tradition of the sea, the last man off the stricken steamer was the captain who didn't leave until he was certain all his men had left and that the ship's situation was utterly hopeless.

Ashore, the weary survivors looked on as the bow of the MONARCH slowly rose to a 50 degree angle and the unmanned engines slowed and stopped. The stern broke off and majestically slipped from the reef. The bow remained fast, occasionally taking the brunt of the crashing sea. The crew turned its attention to the more pressing problem of survival.

A fire was built from driftwood. It helped fight the cold and also served as a signal to either a passing steamer or the lightkeeper at Passage Island. The lake continued to be churned by a moderate gale and no ship was sighted during the day.

Another bitter night came and another gray dawn. Still no hope arrived and still the storm raged.

Living on frozen salmon and flour washed ashore from the wreck, the survivors knew their chances were growing smaller with each passing hour. Cold and without shelter or substantial food, they could not expect to continue for long. Huddled behind a makeshift wind break made from sails salvaged from the wreck, they waited in the freezing weather for whichever was to come first; help. . .or death.

Four men, knowing there was a fishermen's camp at Tobin Harbor a dozen miles to the south, hiked in that direction for help. They found that the cabins had been deserted for the year, but some meager provisions had been left behind. These were added to the survivors' stocks of flour and frozen salmon.

Unknown to the shivering and demoralized survivors, the Passage Island lightkeeper, had sighted the glow from their fire on the 7th, but the stormy seas prevented investigating. All through the 8th, he also saw the flickering signal and anxiously waited for the seas to abate. Finally on the 9th the assistant lightkeeper was able to row over and investigate. The trip, over four miles of still rough water, was anything but easy!

Two views of the bow of the MONARCH fast on Blake Point.

Archives, Michigan Department of State

Arriving opposite the fire, the lightkeeper was unable to land in the rolling surf. The steamer's purser, however, bravely swam through the surf to the bobbing boat and related the desperate details. The lightkeeper then made the return trip to the light with the MONARCH's purser. Once there, he was able to hail the outbound steamer EDMONTON which returned to Port Arthur and relayed the news of the disaster.

The EDMONTON arrived in port at 2 a.m. By 6 a.m., the tug JAMES WHALEN was enroute under forced pressure. The four-hour delay was caused by the loading of an extra 20 tons of coal needed for the long trip. The WHALEN's captain climbed out of his sick bed to run the tug. He had time to be sick later. Right now he was badly needed to rescue the MONARCH survivors. Also aboard were two doctors. They were pulled from warm beds and bundled on the tug in case the survivors needed medical care.

Medical supplies, food, blankets and heavy rescue gear were stored below. With her blunt bow shouldering aside the gray rollers of a still wild lake, the WHALEN made a difficult heavy weather crossing.

When the tug arrived opposite the wreck at 10 a.m. the surf was still too high to make a landing. Blowing her steam whistle to signal her intentions, the WHALEN churned her way around Blake's Point and south to calmer waters in the island's lee. There she landed a rescue party which hiked to the survivors' camp.

When the battered and utterly exhausted survivors reached the WHALEN, they were found to be suffering from various degrees of exposure and frostbite. But they were alive. And that was a tribute to the courage and seamanship of the Passage Island lightkeeper and the tug WHALEN. For his part in the rescue, deckhand McCollum was awarded a medal by the Royal Humane Society.

The Northern Navigation Company paid no compensation to the passengers for any personal articles lost in the wreck. The company simply considered such a loss to be a risk of lake travel. It did, however, pay for their passage on another steamer.

Proud as a peacock, the steamer MONARCH when she was the "pride of the line".

Runge Collection

Of Canadian registry, the 240-foot, 2,017 gross ton MONARCH was owned by the Northern Navigation Company (Beatty Line) of Sarnia, Ontario, She was built by the Dyble Yard at Sarnia in 1888 and commissioned in 1890 as a wooden package steamer with a value of $150,000. From the beginning she was the "Pride of the Line" and the flagship of the Northern Navigation Fleet.

No effort had been spared in making her one of the finest ships on the lakes. Every detail was attended to during her construction. Her cabin doors were carefully fitted so a coin could slip between the door and frame. Her main saloon was finished with the careful taste of a fine designer. For 15 years she carried passengers in a splendor usually associated with the great Atlantic packets. Her menus and the social events held in her fancy saloons made news in the society pages of the midwest newspapers.

The tug JAMES WHALEN cutting through thick ice in May of 1912 at Port Arthur.

Rutherford B. Hayes Library

Although some salvage efforts were made immediately after the wreck, the MONARCH lay virtually undisturbed for several years until Great Lakes salvor Tom Reid and diver Louis Meyer worked with the tugs GEORGE H. PARKER, SALVOR and OTTAWA and the barge KILDERHOUSE to remove the MONARCH's engines and boilers. The famous salvor reported locating the stern in 90 feet of water and the bow on the shore.

As a point of pittifoggerish interest, only a year previous to the wreck, the MONARCH was converted from a passenger steamer to a freighter. On her last trip as a passenger carrier, wrecker Reid made a point of being aboard.

Exactly why the MONARCH wrecked has never been answered. That Captain Robertson lost his bearings is obvious, but the reason remains unknown. After the wreck he said, "the compass was rendered useless by the cold." This condition, coupled with a more southerly drift than was anticipated, and/or a local magnetic deviation sheds some light on the possible cause for the grounding.

Running on her collision course to Blake's Point, the MONARCH must have passed very near to both Canoe Rocks and the then unnamed Congdon Shoal. It was fortunate she struck on the point rather than either of these deadly reefs. Had she run into either reef, there would have been no survivors. The survivors experienced extreme difficulty reaching shore from 25 feet away. They could never have managed from a mile and a quarter.

Much "treasure" including china plates, cups, silverware and a silver tea service, has been recovered by scuba divers. The capstan has also been salvaged and is on display at the old Rock Harbor Lighthouse. Little is left of the once proud vessel. Bare ribs, lonely hull planks and iron fasteners tell a silent tale. Her huge anchor is wedged between several large rocks and is located in shallow water at the foot of the rock cliffs. The field of wreckage begins a mere 10 yards from the rock cliff in 30 feet of water and extends out into more than 90 feet.

One of the oddities of the MONARCH episode concerns the numerous beer bottles littered throughout the wreck. Most are filled with grain! Over the years many explanations have been advanced as to how and why the grain was in the bottles. Most dealt with some form of smuggling and none have a ring of truth.

The best answer to this minor mystery involves the activities of wrecker Tom Reid. Reid, with his small wrecking fleet, spent a long time on the site while salvaging the MONARCH engines. Reid's wreckers undoubtedly consumed a fair amount of beer and in the days before anti-litter laws, they simply heaved the "dead soldiers" overboard.

The empty bottles eventually worked their way into the wreck and into the grain cargo. They were slowly filled with grain during the process. The loose grain has long since decayed, but that in the bottles remains.

The MONARCH's Chief Engineer, Samuel Beatty, was an old hand at shipwreck. Only the year before he had been the Chief Engineer of the steamer MONK-SHAVEN when she wrecked on Pie Island at the mouth of Thunder Bay on November 28. As in the MONARCH wreck, the survivors also suffered greatly before rescue.

The same storm that wrecked the MONARCH drove another Northern Navigation Company vessel, the IONIC ashore near Whitefish Point, in eastern lake Superior. The fates smiled on the IONIC, however. On December 11 she was hauled free without serious damage.

On December 15, 1906, the Canadian Registration was officially closed. The MONARCH now lives only in the minds and hearts of those divers who brave Superior's frigid depths and the historians who search her dusty history.

BIBLIOGRAPHY

Barry, James P. "SHIPS OF THE GREAT LAKES." Berkley: Howell-North Books, 1910.

Barry, James P. "The Wreck of the Steamer MONARCH." INLAND SEAS, spring, 1980.

Brown, W. Russel. "Ships at Port Arthur and Fort William." INLAND SEAS, October, 1945.

Carus, Captain Edward. "100 Years of Disasters on the Great Lakes." Unpublished manuscript, 1931.

Correspondence from Canadian Department of Transport, September 14, 1973.

"DAILY MINING GAZETTE" (Houghton). December 13, 1906; December 11, 1971.

"DAILY TIMES JOURNAL" (Fort William, Ontario). December 10, 11, 12, 17, 1906.

Dominion of Canada, Department of Marine. "Casualties to Vessels Resulting in Total Loss on the Great Lakes—From 1870 to Date," 1975.

Doner, Mary F. The Salvager. Minneapolis: Ross and Haines, 1958.

"DULUTH NEWS TRIBUNE," December 16, 1906.

"JOURNAL OF THE LIGHT-STATION AT PASSAGE ISLAND." December 6 - 10, 1906. National Archives: Washington, D.C.

Landon, Fred. "Shipwrecks on Isle Royale," "INLAND SEAS," spring, 1960.

Law, W.H. "Deeds of Valor by Heros and Heroines of the Great Water World." Manuscript in Chynoweth Collection, Michigan Technological University Archives.

Mason, George C. "A List of the Hulls Built by F.W. Wheeler and Company." "INLAND SEAS," October, 1945.

Mills, J.C. "OUR INLAND SEAS." Chicago: A.C. McClurg, 1910.

Mills, John M. "CANADIAN COASTAL AND INLAND STEAM VESSELS 1809 - 1930." Providence, Rhode Island: Steamship Historical Society of America, 1979.

Wells, Homer C. "History of Accidents, Casualties and Wrecks on Lake Superior." Duluth, Minnesota: U.S. Army Corps of Engineers, District Engineer Office, Duluth, Minnesota.

VanderLinden Rev., Ed. "GREAT LAKES SHIPS WE REMEMBER," Cleveland: Freshwater Press, 1979.

Williams, W.R. "Shipwrecks at Isle Royale." "INLAND SEAS," winter, 1956.

Wolff, Julius F. "Shipwrecks of Lake Superior, 1900 - 1909" "INLAND SEAS," winter, 1971,

DANIEL B. MEACHEM

The 530 foot steamer D.B. MEACHEM was upbound for Port Arthur on July 28, 1908 with a full cargo of 9,000 tons of coal when, through an error in navigation, she slammed hard on a Passage Island reef. Since the steamer was only several weeks old, it was an ominous beginning for her career!

One of the largest vessels on the lakes, the MEACHEM was owned by the Frontier Steamship Company of Tonawanda, New York and mastered by Captain Deringer. The good Captain was quickly replaced.

The steamer was hauled free by the Canada Towing and Wrecking Company. The famous Duluth wrecker Captain Kidd was at the salvage site, but since it wasn't his job, he only watched. The salvors did a good job of it, but repairs still totaled $40,000.

One might question why the salvors even bothered to pull her off. Three months later, on October 24, downbound from Superior to Ashtabula with ore, she struck on a reef 12 miles north of the Upper Entry, Portage Lake Ship Canal. The JAMES WHALEN had her free in two days, but repairs reached $85,000. It was a tough first year for the MEACHEM!

BIBLIOGRAPHY

"ANNUAL REPORT, U.S. LIFE-SAVING SERVICE 1908." Washington D.C.
"DULUTH NEWS-TRIBUNE," July 30, October 25, 28, November 7, 1908.

OTTAWA

The 256 foot steel hulled Canadian steamer Ottawa was bound down from Fort William on November 15, 1909 when she fell afoul of the storm gods. Carrying a cargo of wheat, this package freighter with her crew of 18 challenged the true fury of a maddened lake and lost!

The OTTAWA, 2,431 tons, 256 feet long and 43 feet in beam, was built in Toronto by the Canadian Shipbuilding Company. She was owned by the Atlantic Railway Company.

When the OTTAWA pulled away from the dock in the early hours of November 13, a strong northwest wind was blowing. Clearing the cut between Passage Island and Isle Royale, the steamer was overtaken by a building northwest sea. With a northwest sea, the further the OTTAWA ran and the further she got from land, the greater the sea. She carried no radio. They were too new for a lowly freighter!

The mate, W.J. Moles, suggested to the Captain, Alex Birnie, that the OTTAWA turn back for shelter and wait for better weather. Ignoring the mates concern, the Captain kept the OTTAWA stubbornly on course.

Heavily loaded, the steamer was frequently awash with the surging waves. About twenty miles east of Passage Island, overstressed by the power of the seas, the shafting connection between the steering gear in the wheelhouse and the steering engine aft became jammed and the OTTAWA was thrown into the trough of the tumbling seas. Slowly, but inexorably, her wheat cargo shifted.

For the next twelve hours, the crew worked deep in the cargo holds, desperately trying to shovel the wheat back into trim. It was a hopeless job.

Exposed more and more to the sweeping seas, the OTTAWA's decks leaked a deluge of water. Although the pumps were at first able to keep up, they soon were overwhelmed. Battered by the pounding seas, the OTTAWA's deckhouses were smashed to pieces.

Urged by the Mate, Captain Birnie ordered his ship abandoned about 10 a.m. on November 15. The fight to save her had been long, but impossible. Captain Birnie and all of the crew successfully left the OTTAWA in the lifeboat.

The crewless ship drifted on for a short time, giving substance to the Captain's belief that she wouldn't sink. Then a series of killer waves battered the beleaguered vessel. Rolling back and forth in the deadly trough of the seas, a spar broke loose and fell across her whistle cord causing her powerful steam whistle to scream loudly in an eerie death wail.

With her whistle still blowing, the OTTAWA plunged stern first beneath the stormy seas. Her bow lifted 50 feet clear of the water. From the wave-tossed lifeboat the Mate noticed the OTTAWA did not go straight down, but rather glided underwater for several hundred yards. Her path was clearly marked by escaping air bubbles.

Although Captain Birnie had lost his ship, he didn't lose his seamanship, courage or leadership. With only a small hand compass and searchlight, he guided the lifeboat over 50 miles of gale churned and snow-blinded lake to safety at the Keweenaw Peninsula's Copper Harbor. All the way the survivors rowed and bailed, and shivered uncontrollably from the piercing cold. After 16 hours of rowing, the lifeboat slipped through the tight Copper Harbor entrance and safely landed on the beach about dawn on the 16th. Dog tired and snow covered, the men and their clothing were actually frozen stiff as a result of the wave spume.

Since only two of the 18 survivors were capable of moving, they went for help. Awakened to the disaster, the townspeople quickly responded and carried the bedraggled victims to their homes. There the half-frozen men were warmed and fed. A special call went out for a doctor and in response a Dr. Kirton came up by special train from the mining town of Phoenix. He found some of the sailor's legs were so badly swollen from exposure to the frigid water, they could not stand. With the good Doctor's help, all eventually recovered.

On November 18th, the crew was taken to Calumet by sleigh, there to be transferred to a train for the trip home. The Mate went on to continue a long sailing career, eventually retiring as a Captain. Captain Birnie, however, retired to his farm and never went to sea again!

BIBLIOGRAPHY

"DAILY MINING GAZETTE" (Houghton, Michigan). November 17, 18, 1909.

"DULUTH NEWS-TRIBUNE." November 17, 18, 1909.

"SUPERIOR TELEGRAM" (Superior, Wisconsin). November 17, 18, 1909.

Mills, John M. "CANADIAN COASTAL AND INLAND STEAM VESSELS 1809 - 1930." Providence, Rhode Island: Steamship Historical Society of America. 1979.

Thom, Robert W. "The Sinking of the OTTAWA." "INLAND SEAS." Winter, 1953.

Wolff, Julius F. "Canadian Shipwrecks of Lake Superior," "INLAND SEAS." Fall, 1978.

THE BRANSFORD, AT
ISLE ROYALE . . . AGAIN

While upbound for Duluth on November 16, 1909, the large steel steamer BRANSFORD ran hard aground on a shoal at the entrance to Siskiwit Bay. The explanation for the stranding was extremely simple. Caught in a gale and blinding blizzard, Captain A.C. Winvig became confused about his true position. He thought he was 11 miles south of Isle Royale and in a safe part of the lake. The possibility of a local magnetic deviation affecting his compass and contributing to the stranding cannot be ignored.

This particular gale caused a host of problems. The OTTAWA was sunk east of Passage Island, the JAMES S. DUNHAM driven on the beach at Marble Point, the CORALIA ashore at the Keweenaw's Bete Gris and the fish tug CITY OF TWO HARBORS ashore east of Superior.

The BRANSFORD suffered fairly heavy damage, but her injuries were scant compared with those of the HARLEM. The BRANSFORD was eventually hauled off after a week of work by the wreckers, led by the Canadian tug JAMES WHALEN and the powerful wrecking tug FAVORITE. After the yard workers finished with the steamer, the repair bills totaled $25,000. It was a costly reacquaintance for the steamer.

The reef she struck has since been Brandsford Reef in her honor. Notice, however, that the name has been misspelled from the original BRANSFORD to "Brandsford."

Four years earlier in November of 1905, when under the command of Captain Balfour, the BRANSFORD had another fatal collision with Isle Royale. She was upbound for Superior in ballast when a classic gale attacked her. For 36 hours she was in the midst of a raging storm of such ferocity that the Mate later commented, "In my 21 years of sailing on the Great Lakes, I never experienced such a storm."

Nearly out of control and in the trough of mountainous seas, the steamer was blown onto a reef off the east shore of Isle Royale. Just when things looked the blackest, and before the Captain could take any action, a wave lifted her off the rocks and deposited her in deep water. Had she been fully loaded with an ore cargo, she likely would not have come off the reef, ever! Limping badly and taking on a lot of water, she continued on course for Superior. She eventually arrived in near to sinking condition. Repairs topped $20,000 and required the replacement of 27 punctured hull plates and attention to four dozen cracked frames. The same gale drove the large steamer MATAAFA on the beach off the Duluth Ship Canal and literally destroyed her.

The 434 foot steamer BRANSFORD, twice a victim of Isle Royales rocks.

Author's Collection

The BRANSFORD also caused a shipwreck. In the wee hours of the morning of November 7, 1902, she ran down the 68 foot tug RECORD in Superior harbor. One of the small tugs crewmen died as the result of injuries suffered in the accident.

Built in 1902 in West Bay City, the BRANSFORD was 434 feet long, 50 feet in the beam and 4,657 gross tons. She was originally operated by the W.A. Hawgood Company of Cleveland. In 1916 she was renamed the JOHN H. MCLEAN and in 1943 was transferred as the CLIFFORD F. HOOD to the American Steel and Wire Company and converted to a craneship.

The old ship was laid up in 1971 and finally towed to Spanish ship breakers in 1974. An ignoble, but typical end for a once-proud laker.

BIBLIOGRAPHY

Bowen, Dana Thomas. "MEMORIES OF THE LAKES," Cleveland: Freshwater Press, 1969.

Dowling, Rev. Edward J. "The Tin Stackers, The Story of the Ships of the Pittsburgh Steel Company," "INLAND SEAS," spring, 1954.

"DULUTH NEWS TRIBUNE," December 21, 1905.

"EVENING TELEGRAM" (Superior, Wisconsin). November 18, 19, 24, 1909.

"FORT WILLIAM DAILY TIMES-JOURNAL." November 18, 1909.

Holden, Thom R. "Park Interpretation as an Environmental Communication Process With a Sample Interpretive Booklet Text on the Maritime Disasters History of Siskiwit Bay, Isle Royale, Lake Superior," unpublished master's thesis, University of Wisconsin - Madison, 1974.

"MERCHANT VESSELS OF THE UNITED STATES," various issues.

Sykes, Allen. "Clifford F. Hood in Retrospect," "THE NOR'EASTER," January - February, 1981.

Wells, Homer C. "History of Accidents, Casualties and Wrecks on Lake Superior," U.S. Army Corps of Engineers, 1938. Typewritten manuscript in District Engineers Office.

Wolff, Julius F. "The Shipwrecks of Lake Superior, 1900 - 1909," "INLAND SEAS," spring, 1972.

THE DUNELM'S DEADLINE

The steel steamer DUNELM was built by the Sunderland Shipbuilding Company, Sunderland, England in 1907. Like the steamer KEMLOOPS, the DUNELM was a "canaler," a vessel whose size was limited by the dimensions of the Welland Canal.

Still, at 250 feet in length, 43 feet in beam, 23.5 feet in depth and 2,319 gross registered tons, she was a hefty ship. After a rough Atlantic crossing, the steamer began service under the flag of the Inland Navigation Company.

Early evening of December 6, 1910 found her tied to her Port Arthur grain dock. She had finished loading her 105,000 bushels of wheat and flour cargo and seemed to be in no hurry to sail. At 10 p.m. she was still tied up and by 10:30 there was no movement at all. Since the vessel's insurance expired at midnight, her behavior was very strange.

Finally, at 11:30, in the company of the 410 foot steamer F.B. SQUIRE, she began to get underway. . .only minutes before her insurance deadline!

Both vessels had soon passed Thunder Cape and were out in the open lake. A thick blizzard with a frost fog had destroyed visibility and a heavy sea was running, making the going rough for both steamers. Steering by compass, they headed for Passage Island, intending to use it as a final reference point for the trip to the Soo. Trapped in the blizzard and tossed by the seas, they were unable to find Passage Island and lost track of their position. They elected to return to Thunder Bay and wait for better weather.

While working their way back, the DUNELM ran hard up on Canoe Rocks, just 7,500 feet off Isle Royale's west shore. The SQUIRE, slightly seaward of the DUN-

ELM, was in deep water and avoided the shoal. Equipped with a wireless, a new-fangled device not installed on the DUNELM, the SQUIRE wired Port Arthur and advised them of the accident. To the master of the SQUIRE the DUNELM didn't appear to be in any immediate danger so he proceeded on his way.

The DUNELM fast on Canoe Rocks.

University of Detroit

Aboard the stranded steamer, Captain Albinson, a master for many years, did all he could to determine the extent of his ship's damage. He discovered that she was punctured badly and taking water through scores of rent plates, and although she rested firmly on the rocks and wasn't in immediate danger of sinking, she wasn't in any place to await rescue!

At 10 a.m. Albinson ordered his two lifeboats lowered, secured his vessel's official papers and had his crew gather warm clothing. Rowing through the cresting seas, the two boats reached the shore safely and landed on the beach of Duncan Bay. Winter ice had already begun to form on the rocks along the coast which made it difficult for the crew to climb to the plateau above the beach.

The captain ordered that a bonfire be built. It would give warmth and serve as a beacon.

After being "thawed out" by the blaze, the captain, the mate, several engineers and the wheelsman returned to the DUNELM for additional supplies. They were back in a few hours with a boatload of blankets and supplies.

Shipwreck on Lake Superior was old hat for Albinson. He had been aboard the Algoma Central Railway steamer MONKSHAVEN when she was trapped in the great gale of November, 1905. Caught in the trough of those merciless seas, she was thrown on the rocks at Pie Island near Port Arthur and totally destroyed.

The tug JAMES WHALEN eventually responded to SQUIREs' wireless message and steamed bravely into sight, brushing aside waves just as she had when she came to rescue the MONARCH's survivors four years earlier.

Under the tow of the tug BOWAN the DUNELM arrives in Port Arthur on Christmas Day 1910.

Lake Superior Marine Museum

The DUNELM's crew signaled to her with flares and fired a beacon made from a bed sheet soaked with coal oil. The WHALEN saw the pyrotechnic display and responded. When the tug determined that the crew was in no immediate danger, she decided to shelter at nearby Silver Islet and wait for the heavy seas to calm down. When conditions improved the next day, the WHALEN returned and anchored in a small bay several miles from the campsite. The crew used lifeboats to row down to the rescue.

Advised of the DUNLEM's condition, her owners turned her over to the insurance underwriters, who in turn gave the salvage job to the Canadian Towing and Wrecking Company. The salvors went to work quickly. If the DUNELM was to be saved, it had to be done immediately.

They worked day and night. Again and again the clam bucket of the barge EMPIRE dug deeply into the steamer's grain cargo in an attempt to lighten the ship. Huge steam pumps were hoisted aboard and, clanking and wheezing, they began the job of "dewatering" her. Chances of saving the DUNELM were considered small, especially in view of the lateness of the season. Time and again the wreckers were driven off the steamer by gales. Each time they returned. . .more tenacious than ever!

Ice was a constant problem. It clogged pumps and turned the decks to sheets of glass. The ship's weight had become enormous. The longer the DUNELM sat on the reef the more ice formed. More than 400 tons were eventually chopped off and thrown overboard.

To the outside world the DUNELM was a dead ship. She surely could not be saved. But the salvors surprised everyone. On December 21, their toil was rewarded. Responding to the grunting and straining of the salvage tugs, the steamer came to life, slid noisily off the reef and floated free.

Because the DUNELM was in no condition for a lengthy tow, the tugs brought her into the nearby shallows of Duncan Bay. There a temporary patch was applied to her wounds.

The "patching" of a steel vessel is fascinating. The patch itself is made of wood, canvas and cement or any combination of the three. When applied over the hole area, the patch takes the place of the missing hull. It is strictly temporary, though, and intended to last only until the vessel is brought to drydock. The usual procedure calls for a "hard hat" diver to drill a series of fastening holes around the area to receive the patch. He then builds a template to fit the drilled holes. Topside, using the template as a guide, a patch is constructed of wooden planks and canvas. The patch is lowered over the side and bolted over the hole at pre-drilled holes. Everything is then covered with a special cement mixture to assure some degree of watertightness. When pumped out, the ship should float.

The salvage fleet hard at work on the DUNELM in Duncan Bay.

K.E. Thro Collection

By 6:30 Christmas morning, repairs had been completed. Under the tow of the tug BOWAN, the DUNELM headed for Port Arthur nearly 40 miles away. During the trip some of the patches on the vessel began to loosen. When she reached the CNR dock at one in the afternoon, additional pumps were required to hold the leaks in check.

The DUNELM after being salvaged and incorporated into the Canada Steamship Lines.

Runge Collection,
Milwaukee Public Library

The arrival of the DUNELM created a fair amount of excitement. The citizens of the Thunder Bay area had anxiously followed the drama via wireless from the salvage tugs. When the tugs finally brought her in, many people went out to watch. Many a Christmas dinner was interrupted by the arrival of the scarred and battered DUNELM.

The work of the Canadian Towing and Wrecking Company was a complete and unqualified success. Not only was the fine ship saved from the lake, but over half her cargo was salvaged.

Two views of the DUNELM in her Port Arthur drydock.
Note the huge amounts of water pouring out of the punctured hull plates.

Lake Superior Marine Museum

The salvors had taken a tremendous financial risk. During the latter phase of the operation they'd worked under the pressure of a "no cure, no pay" contract. The entire operation was directed by Captain James Morrison. When the DUNELM arrived in Port Arthur, Morrison heaved a sigh of relief and called her "the best Christmas box of the season."[1]

Final repairs to the DUNELM were made in Port Arthur's new drydock. Just completed, the drydock hosted the steamer as its first occupant.

The DUNELM's story wasn't over. Through various amalgamations, the Inland Lines became part of the Canada Steamship Lines. After the start of World War I, the CSL sent the DUNELM out to sail salt water. She disappeared on a voyage from Sidney to England on December 6, 1915.

FOOTNOTES

1. *"FORT WILLIAM MORNING HERALD," December 26, 1910.*

BIBLIOGRAPHY

Brady, Edward M. *"MARINE SALVAGE OPERATIONS."* Cambridge, Maryland: Cornell Maritime Press, 1960.

"DAILY MINING GAZETTE" (Houghton). *December 9, 10, 11, 1910.*

"DULUTH NEWS-TRIBUNE." December 10, 12, 21, 1910.

"Journal of the Light-Station at Passage Island." December 1 - 21, 1910. National Archives, Washington D.C.

Mills, John M. *"CANADIAN COASTAL AND INLAND STEAM VESSELS, 1809 - 1930."* Providence, Rhode Island: Steamship Historical Society of America, 1979.

Morrison, Neil F. *"The Rescue of the DUNELM."* Unpublished manuscript in Chynoweth Collection, Michigan Technological University Archives, undated.

"PORT ARTHUR DAILY NEWS" (Ontario). *December 7, 8, 12, 13, 14, 19, 22, 23, 24, 27, 1910; January 7, 14, 21, 1911.*

Sanderson, Herbert Eugene. *"PICTORIAL MARINE HISTORY."* Sturgeon Bay, Wisconsin.

Williams, W.R. *"Shipwrecks at Isle Royale." "INLAND SEAS,"* winter, 1956.

NORTHERN QUEEN

The grasping claws of the Rock of Ages Reef have tickled the bottoms of many vessels. Some, like the CUMBERLAND, COX and CHISHOLM with deadly results. One of the ships that escaped the reef was the NORTHERN QUEEN.

The 300 foot steel steamer of the Mutual Transit Company was downbound on September 10, 1913 when she ran up on a shelf of Rock of Ages Reef. Two days later the tugs JAMES WHALEN and HORNE with the barge EMPIRE, lightered part of her cargo and hauled her free. Taken to Port Arthur, her bottom was found to be damaged badly and repairs were estimated at $20,000.

The NORTHERN QUEEN had several earlier scrapes with trouble. On December 3, 1906, a north gale blew her ashore at Point Abbaye, Michigan, but she was recovered without undue effort. On July 29, 1901, while in a thick Whitefish Bay fog, she rammed the 308 foot whaleback barge SAGAMORE sinking her off Point Iroquois.

BIBLIOGRAPHY

"DAILY MINING GAZETTE" (Houghton). September 13, 1913.
"MARQUETTE MINING JOURNAL." September 11, 12, 1913.

THE 'CONGDON'
OF CONGDON SHOAL

Just eight years after Canoe Rocks nearly claimed the steamer DUNELM, a shoal just 1,500 feet to the southwest laid permanent claim to the steamer CHESTER A. CONGDON. The steel bulk carrier CONGDON, official number 204526, was built in South Chicago in 1907 by the Chicago Steam Boat Company. Originally named the SALT LAKE CITY, the 6,530 gross ton vessel was huge: 532 feet in length, 56.2 feet in beam and 26.5 feet in depth. Her proud owner was the Home Steam Ship Company, but she was managed by the W.A. Hawgood Company of Cleveland. The SALT LAKE CITY was purchased in April, 1912 by the Continental Steamship Company of Duluth and renamed the CHESTER A. CONGDON.

The 525 foot, 6,530 ton CHESTER A. CONGDON steaming through the Duluth Canal.

K.E. Thro Collection

84

The CONGDON departed Fort Williams at 2:28 a.m., November 6, 1918 under Captain Charles Autterson. She was downbound with a cargo of 380,000 bushels of Canadian wheat. By the time she had steamed past Thunder Cape, a heavy sea was running and a southwest wind was blowing a gale. At 4:00, she came about and anchored to wait for better weather.

By 10:15 the next morning the sea and wind had let up and the CONGDON was underway again. But outside the Cape a death-still fog had set in and visibility was very, very bad.

Passing Thunder Bay Cape at 10:40, the steamer set a course for Passage Island and adjusted her speed to nine miles per hour. The CONGDON intended to run for two and a half hours and, if the fog still persisted, stop and wait for clearer weather.

Had the steamer kept her course for the intended time she would have stopped short of Passage Island, but she strayed south and 2½ hours was long enough to reach Canoe Rocks. At 1:30 p.m. on November 7, the CONGDON ran hard up on the shoal that now bears her name. When the weather moderated, the Chief Engineer took a lifeboat back to Thunder Bay for help.

Although the steamer was badly damaged, there was a chance to save her if the salvors could work quickly and the weather held. It wasn't to be. The lake had been cheated in 1910 when the DUNELM pulled from its grasp. The lake would not lose again.

Wreckers arrived from Port Arthur with the barge EMPIRE, a veteran of the DUNELM salvage, within hours of the stranding. Working desperately, they lightered a small portion of her wheat cargo before a 55-mile-an-hour southeast gale drove them and the crew off the wreck and into the shelter of an Isle Royale bay.

When the wreckers returned, they discovered the gale had ravaged the steamer unmercifully. The once proud CONGDON had broken in two at the number six hatch and the aft portion had slipped partly underwater. The bow was still on the surface, but heavily damaged and swinging precariously on the rocks. The situation was extremely dangerous, but the wreckers continued to salvage what they could.

The CONGDON, abandoned by her owners as a total loss, was immediately purchased for $10,000 by James Playfair, a noted Great Lakes marineman. It turned out to be a bad gamble!

When Playfair's crew reached the wreck site, the steamer was gone. The lake broke clean over the shoal; not a speck of the CHESTER A. CONGDON remained.

At that time, the sinking of the CONGDON was the greatest loss (both in money and tonnage) ever suffered on the Great Lakes. Vessel and cargo were valued at 1½ million. Part of the reason for the high loss was the inflated value of the wheat cargo ($2.35 per bushel). World War I commodity prices were sky high.

Until the CONGDON disaster, the dubious distinction of being the largest steamer lost on the lakes belonged to the steamer HENRY B. SMITH. The SMITH disappeared in Lake Superior during the great blow of November, 1913.[1] The SMITH was 525 feet long and had a 10,000 ton capacity. The CONGDON measured 532 feet and 10,400 tons.

Why the CONGDON strayed south of her course is still open to speculation. Even though all the officers survived, pinning down the blame for the loss of a vessel and cargo can be difficult. Perhaps the most acceptable answer is that a local magnetic attraction was the culprit, a common problem near Isle Royale.

From examining her article book, it is evident that the CONGDON carried a large crew. On her last trip 36 men were aboard.[2] Several times during the 1918 season, the crew reached 38. During her last trip, the 19th of the season, she carried four apprentices. The apprentices were paid a nominal salary of one dollar a month. The men they were apprenticed under received normal pay. A wheelsman or fireman received $100 a month and the engineers were paid $149.50.

As with any major lakes vessel, the CONGDON throughout her life had numerous scrapes. On May 31, 1918, she grazed the 504 foot GEORGE G. BARNUM in a

Whitefish Bay fog. Damages to both ships were only slight. Earlier in her career she suffered $20,000 in damages when after losing her way in a Lake Michigan fog, she ran hard up on a rock reef near Bailey's Harbor on the Door Peninsula. This accident could have ended her career except for two events: she was running light (with water ballast only) and after dewatering was able to back free. A patrolling surfman spotted the lights of the steamer heading for the beach and warned her off with a coston flare. However, since she was running at full speed (12 mph), she could not stop quickly enough. Nonetheless, she was able to slow her speed. Had she not seen the flare and checked her speed and not been in water ballast, she could have finished her days as a Lake Michigan wreck instead of a Superior one.

The CONGDON as the SALT LAKE CITY.

Dossin Great Lakes Institute

The following four views are of the CONGDON on the shoal. Consider the tremendous force that literally snapped her in two!

Lake Superior Marine Museum

A graphic illustration of the extreme underwater topography of Isle Royale is this sonar tracing of Congdon Shoal. One minute the vessel is in water hundreds of feet deep, the next she's aground.

Right Here II

The CONGDON is an exciting experience for a diver. The bow, with the pilothouse intact, is east of the shoal and standing upright in 110 feet of water. Alone, without the rest of the vessel, she presents a most unusual appearance.

The wreckage of the aft portion is resting on the west side of the shoal and starts in approximately 20 feet of water. Following the wreckage down the shoal the diver will reach the stern in 180 feet. The entire aft section is at an angle of approximately 65 degrees.

The shallow part of the vessel is a scene of complete and utter destruction. Bent and twisted steel plates and bracing are everywhere. Steel plates have been torn and crumpled like paper. Deeper down the hull, the vessel resumes some semblance of order, although thousands of popped rivets are in the hold, further evidence of the destructive power of the lake. At approximately 60 feet

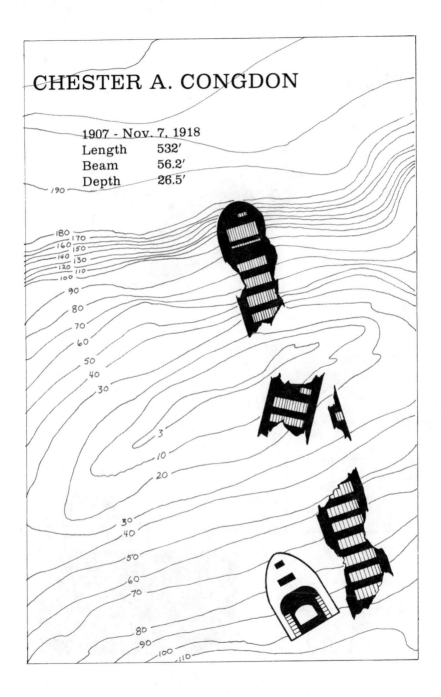

CHESTER A. CONGDON

1907 - Nov. 7, 1918
Length 532'
Beam 56.2'
Depth 26.5'

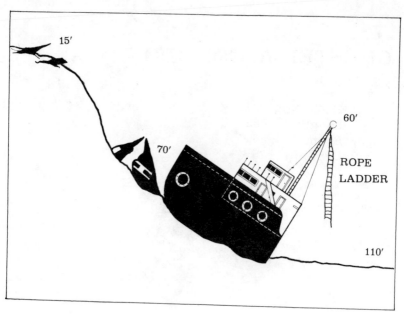

A sketch showing the present underwater layout of the CONGDON.

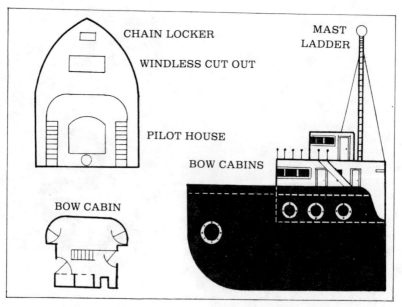

the vessel is comparatively intact and remains so through to the stern cabin.

As a diver swims down the wreck his sense of anxiety grows each foot he descends. The bright yellows and greens of the shallow water have slowly given way to darker greens and browns. Visibility has also gradually decreased. Near the surface one can see 60 feet or more. At the stern visibility of 15 feet would be good. The gloom that once kept at arm's length now presses in like a weight. It's dark, cold and just plain spooky, but the CONGDON is wreck diving at its best.

FOOTNOTES

1. The term "disappeared" is used advisedly.

2. The crew was required to officially sign on at the start of each trip and off at the end. This was done in a book known as the "article book."

BIBLIOGRAPHY

"ANNUAL REPORT OF THE LAKE CARRIERS ASSOCIATION," 1918.
"ANNUAL REPORT OF THE UNITED STATES LIFE-SAVING SERVICE." U.S. Government Printing Office: Washington, D.C.
Article Book, steamer CHESTER A. CONGDON, 1918.
Carus, Captain Edward. "100 Years of Disasters on the Great Lakes." Unpublished manuscript, 1931.
"Consolidated Certificate of Enrollment and License, Steamer CHESTER A. CONGDON."
"GREAT LAKES PILOT." U.S. Department of Commerce, 1973.
"MERCHANT VESSELS OF THE U.S.," various issues.
"NEWS CHRONICLE" (Port Arthur). November 8, 9, December 13, 1918.
"NEW YORK TIMES." November 10, 1918.
Wicklund, Richard H. "Largest Lakers Lost, 1913 - 1975." "TELESCOPE." September - October, 1977.
Wolff, Julius F. "THE SHIPWRECKS OF LAKE SUPERIOR." Duluth: Lake Superior Marine Museum, 1979.

THE STRANGER OF MENAGERIE

With deliberate purpose, the Great Lakes Transportation Company steamer GLENLYON worked its way through the storm-tossed lake, her steel bow neatly slicing through the oncoming waves. It was Thursday, October 30, 1924, and she was downbound from Fort Williams to Port Colborne with a cargo of 145,000 bushels of golden Canadian wheat. The GLENLYON made good progress, but the storm was growing more violent.

To avoid punishing his vessel, Captain Taylor brought her back into Thunder Bay and the shelter of the Welcome Islands. He hid there all day Friday, leaving to resume his trip only after the gale had let up.

After a rough fall storm, the GLENLYON entered port with a thick coat of ice.

Dossin Great Lakes Institute

But the captain was lured into a nefarious Lake Superior trap! Once the GLENLYON had passed Passage Island, the supposedly dying gale lashed at the steamer with renewed fury. Heavily beset, the GLENLYON could no longer continue. Taylor brought the steamer around and headed for the shelter of Siskiwit Bay. Like the CENTURION, BRANSFORD and HARLEM, she looked for the calm waters of a safe anchorage but found, instead, the jagged rock of an outlying reef. The shoal she struck is located ¾ miles north of Menagerie Island and is now called Glenlyon Shoal.

An immediate SOS was tapped out by the radio operator when the GLENLYON fetched up. The message was received by numerous stations including the vessels GLENLINNIE of the Glen Line and GLENSANNOX also owned by the Great Lakes Transportation Company. Both steamers headed quickly for their stricken sister.

The GLENLYON was in rough shape. Water was pouring through rock-torn holes and she was flooding badly. The engine room had flooded completely and the entire length of the steamer was forced on the reef. She was now fully exposed to the gale. To avoid being pounded to pieces, Taylor ordered the sea cocks opened and flooded the steamer firmly down on the rocks.

With the GLENLINNIE and GLENSANNOX lying just off the wreck in deep water, Taylor tried to keep his crew on board until it was safe to transfer. During the confusion of the stranding, however, the first mate and a crewman lowered a lifeboat and left the ship.

They were quickly blown from sight by the roaring gale. Part of the crew later transferred to the GLENSANNOX and was taken down lake. Captain Taylor remained on board with the rest to wait for the salvage crews he was sure would come.

The two missing crewmen were picked up a day later from the Minnesota shore by a Coast Guard cutter. For 15 hours they had a harrowing ride on the edge of the gale. Drenched by cold water and buffeted by winds, both suffered from exposure.[1]

The GLENLYON's original distress signal was received at Port Arthur where the tug STRATHMORE made a hurried 6 a.m. departure.

The JAMES WHALEN and the barge EMPIRE were also underway. As with the DUNELM wreck, any salvage attempt would have to be hasty. But the still rough lake forced the salvors to lay over for a short time at the Welcome Islands.

The U.S. Coast Guard also received the GLENLYON's SOS and mobilized its resources. The Eagle Harbor crew attempted to reach the wreck in their lifeboat but engine trouble forced them to return. The Portage Lake crew eventually reached the GLENLYON after a difficult 50-mile run into the teeth of the gale. For their efforts the crew of both stations were voted a resolution of thanks by the Dominion Marine Association of Canada.

The cutter COOK also departed for the wreck from the Soo, but blew the manifold on her main engine before leaving the St. Mary's River. She left again after hurried repairs and within minutes discovered her flywheel to be damaged. That was enough. She was forced to withdraw from any further rescue attempts. The COOK's participation was further limited by the incredible fact that the Coast Guard had not equipped her with a complete wireless set.

By Sunday, November 2, the salvors were hard at work. The EMPIRE and the barge GREEN RIVER managed to recover 10,000 bushels of wheat before the heavy seas forced them off.

Captain Taylor made a close inspection of his vessel and reported, "the decks were shoved up 20 inches from the number two hatch to the boiler house and a big hole was in the starboard side . . .the engine room floor was also shoved up."[2]

As with the DUNELM, the key element in the salvage operation was the weather. If it remained good the wheat could be lightered and the steamer pumped out and hauled off. But it was fall on Lake Superior, not much of a time to hope for good weather.

But Lake Superior had a reputation for being moody and, surprisingly, the weather remained moderate for several days. The newspapers even began predicting the exact day the GLENLYON would be brought safely to port!

Salvage work continued into November, and it was becoming evident that the steamer was more seriously damaged than had been thought. Most of the wheat was recovered but had to be dried before being resold. Unable, finally, to pull her off, the salvors left the GLENLYON on the reef to battle the winter storms alone.

When the salvors returned in the spring, the GLEN-LYON was not there! The winter ice had forced her off the reef and into deep water. She was a total loss.

For a shallow wreck, the GLENLYON is probably the least explored of any of the Isle Royale wrecks. Resting north of Menagerie Island, the wreck best resembles a peeled banana, with her hull plates bordering the guts of her machinery. The huge engine lays over on its right side. Behind stretches the long prop shaft, at the end of which is the propeller. Just yards away is a spare bucket or blade dropped when the ceaseless storms of Superior tore apart its storage site on the stern deck. Across the reef is what is left of the bow. The winch remains set in her deck and both anchors are still there, one resting on the rock bottom, the other firmly planted on its pocket. By any account, it's a fine diving experience.

The GLENLYON, official number U.S. 81427, Canada 126660, was built in 1893 at West Bay City, Michigan by the F.W. Wheeler Company as a steel package freighter. At 2,818 gross feet in depth. Originally named the WIL-LIAM H. GRATWICK, the vessel was named for a lumber baron with extensive shipping interests. She was sold to the Duluth Transportation Company and renamed the MINNEKAHTA in 1902.

In 1914, she was sold a second time to the Great Lakes Transportation Company and renamed the GLENLYON. Old paint was scraped away and she received her new colors: light blue for the hull, white for the cabins and a light red stack with a jet black top. She was painted this way when she became a "Stranger on Menagerie."

Steamer Glenlyon at Wallaceburg, Canada

A postcard view of the GLENLYON steaming down Canada's Sydenham River.

Runge Collection

FOOTNOTES

1. *It isn't clear as to how the two men came to be adrift. The rumor is that they deserted the GLENLYON fearing she was lost. Captain Taylor however, later stated that they launched the lifeboat to assess the hull damage but were cast adrift when the painter broke. Neither tale has the complete ring of truth. It also isn't clear who picked up the castaways. The first mate claimed it was the Coast Guard, while the Coast Guard records state it was a merchant vessel.*

2. *"DAILY TIMES JOURNAL" (Port Arthur). November 1, 1924.*

BIBLIOGRAPHY

"DAILY TIMES-JOURNAL" (Fort William, Ontario). November 1, 3, 4, 5, 13, 1924.
"DETROIT MARINE HISTORIAN." November, 1978.
"DULUTH NEWS TRIBUNE." November 2, 3, 1924.
"EVENING NEWS" (Sault Ste. Marie, Michigan). November 1, 3, 1924.

Holden, Robert Thomas. "Park Interpretation as an Environmental Communication Process with a Sample Interpretive Booklet Text on the Marine Disaster History of Siskiwit Bay, Isle Royale, Lake Superior." Master's thesis, University of Wisconsin-Madison, 1974.

"MARQUETTE MINING JOURNAL." November 1, 1924.

Mason, George C. "A List of the Hulls Built by F.W. Wheeler and Company." "INLAND SEAS." October, 1945.

"U.S. COAST GUARD DISPATCHES." Number ZA46, November 1, 1924; Number ZA261, November 2, 1924.

"U.S. COAST GUARD REPORT." Subject: attempt to carry out Commander, Lakes Division, Orders, November 1, 1924.

Williams, W.R. "Shipwrecks at Isle Royale." "INLAND SEAS," winter, 1956.

Wright, Richard J. "FRESHWATER WHALES." Kent State University Press, 1969.

MISSING, OFF ISLE ROYALE
(Reprinted from *Went Missing*)[1]

For 50 years the KAMLOOPS remained one of the Lake's great enigmas. She was truly a vessel that "went missing." Like so many of that exclusive club, she left a handful of clues to her fate, but interpreting them had not been easy.

Nonetheless, again and again the experts pondered her fate, and searched and searched. On August 21, 1979, their efforts were successful. The wreck of the long missing KAMLOOPS was discovered. This is her story.

The KAMLOOPS, official number 147682, had been built for the Canada Steamship Lines in 1924 at the Haverton Hill shipyard of the Furness Shipbuilding Company. Constructed of steel, she was 250 feet in length, 42.9 feet in beam, 24.3 feet in depth and 2,402 gross tons. Her single, triple-expansion steam engine could drive her at 9½ knots.

The KAMLOOPS was designed as a package freighter. Her cargo could include nearly every item under the sun, except for bulk cargo of coal or ore. The KAMLOOPS did occasionally carry grain south from Fort William, however.

In Great Lakes jargon she was a "canaler," built to navigate the Welland Canal and therefore limited to the size of the canal. In many respects the canaler was the Great Lakes equivalent of the oceangoing tramp.[2] The KAMLOOPS began her last trip without premonition of disaster. On November 30, 1927, she cleared Hamilton Harbor and after touching at Windsor on December 2, cleared the Soo upbound the following day. Beyond Whitefish Point, however, the lake was churned by a rolling northerly.

100

gale. Captain William Brian, the KAMLOOPS' master, elected to drop anchor behind the point and wait until the weather let up.

Brian, at 45, had already spent 24 years on the lakes and was known as an able navigator. His previous command was the steamer KENORA, another canaler.

When the lake calmed down a bit, the KAMLOOPS hauled anchor and began the long trek to Fort William. Ahead of her by a quarter mile was the Paterson Line steamer QUEDOC, mastered by Roy Simpson.

Aboard the KAMLOOPS was a crew of 20 men and two stewardesses.[3] The KAMLOOPS was not under any deadline, but it was the last trip of the season and the sooner she reached Fort William and received her downbound cargo the better.

Deep in the KAMLOOPS' holds was a varied cargo of 2,115 tons: foodstuffs, general merchandise, wire and a shipment of heavy paper-making machinery consigned to the Thunder Bay Paper Company. The machinery had come from England and was needed for a plant expansion. The holds were to be filled with a large grain cargo on her return trip.

Several hours after leaving Whitefish Point, the vessels encountered heavy weather. Both ships were bucking bow on into a rising northwest gale. Seas as high as the pilothouse roared down on the ships and battered into the steel hulls with pile driver force.

To further complicate the situation, the temperature dropped drastically. Thick ice formed on the decks. Each wave added more ice until both steamers were encumbered by tons of white frosting. Each ship took on the ghostly appearance of a floating ice statue.

The ice also had a terrible side effect. Each added pound changed the ship's center of gravity. If enough ice formed, the delicate balance would be crossed and the ship would capsize from the sheer weight of the ice.

On Tuesday night, December 6, both vessels neared Isle Royale. The QUEDOC was still in the lead and the KAMLOOPS was barely visible a quarter mile astern.

The weather was still wild and both vessels were beleaguered by the heavy seas. The frost fog was also rising
and visibility was awful. The QUEDOC had intended to
make Passage Island around midnight, passing between
it and Isle Royale's Blake Point. This was the usual
vessel track to Fort William.

The KAMLOOPS in her CSL colors before her tragic loss.

Public Archives of Canada

About 10:00 p.m., the QUEDOC's lookout shouted that
he had sighted a "mass of rocks" ahead.[4] The QUEDOC
hauled off to starboard and safely avoided them, but it
was a near miss. The desperate maneuver threw the
QUEDOC dangerously into the trough of the waves
where the overburden of ice nearly capsized her. The
QUEDOC blew her whistle as a warning to the KAM-
LOOPS still following behind, but received no answer.
The QUEDOC lost sight of the KAMLOOPS during the
turn and was never to see her again.

Since the KAMLOOPS had a lower pilothouse than
the QUEDOC, Captain Simpson thought she might have
had greater trouble seeing the rocks in time to avoid
them. But he heard no distress signals and he saw no

distress rockets, so he continued on.

The QUEDOC reached Fort William safely and Captain Simpson thought no more about the KAMLOOPS.

The same gale that Simpson had battled caught several other vessels in its clutches. The steamer E.W. OGLEBAY was blown ashore east of Marquette; the Mathews Line steamer LAMBTON was driven on a reef off Parisienne Island, west of the Soo; and the steamer MARTIAN driven on Hare Island at the mouth of Thunder Bay. Worst of all was the wreck of the Paterson Line steamer ALTADOC, under the command of Captain Dick Simpson, Roy Simpson's brother.

The ALTADOC had been upbound to Fort William when the northwest gale struck her. The waves punished her so fiercely that every piece of gear on deck was swept overboard. The steamer finally lost her steering gear and drifted hopelessly before the gale. With visibility reduced to a bare 200 feet by a snowstorm, the crew was completely unaware of their location, even when the vessel fetched up on a reef. Later, when the weather cleared, they realized they were on Keweenaw Point. Only a few yards away was the wreck of the steamer CITY OF BANGOR which had gone ashore the previous year. The old hull had become a well-known navigational reference point.

Heroic efforts by the Coast Guard led to the rescue of Captain Dick Simpson and his crew. Ice had closed in around the wreck so thickly that the cutter CRAWFORD had to run a path into the ALTADOC. The Coast Guard crew from the Eagle Harbor Station then went through the CRAWFORD's channel in their surfboat to reach the steamer and perform the rescue. The very fact that the Eagle Harbor crew even reached the wrecked ALTADOC is remarkable. To get to the scene they had to travel in a surfboat 22 miles through a raging gale. By the time they had finished the rescue every member of the crew was suffering from frostbite and exposure.

Throughout these days the QUEDOC's captain stood by the Paterson Line Office for any news of his brother. The ALTADOC was his immediate concern, not the KAMLOOPS.

It was of no great concern when the KAMLOOPS became overdue at Fort William. She was almost new, well found and manned by an experienced captain and crew. But the days passed by and still no word was heard from the KAMLOOPS.

When it became obvious that something was seriously wrong a massive search effort was started. Oddly, Captain Simpson, a man with definite information to contribute, didn't mention anything about his KAMLOOPS experience until December 12. On that day he was locking through the Soo and hearing the furor over the missing steamer, he related his experience.

The following morning the Coast Guard at Eagle Harbor received a telegram from the KAMLOOPS' agents asking if the steamer was aground at Keweenaw Point. Having just returned from the area, they replied that she wasn't.

Throughout that afternoon the small Coast Guard Station was deluged with dispatches and long distance telephone calls inquiring about the KAMLOOPS. Had the vessel gone ashore at Manitou Island? Boatswain A.F. Glaza, the Officer in Charge of the Eagle Harbor Station, decided to search the island. The next problem was getting his heavy power lifeboat out of the iced-in harbor!

The lighter power surfboat was better-suited to the task because she could have been dragged over the ice and launched directly into open water.[5] However, during the ALTADOC rescue four forward planks were stoved in and it was not fit for use.

It would also have been easier for the cutter CRAWFORD to make the search, but she had badly damaged her propellers breaking the ice channel during the ALTADOC rescue.

Later, temporarily repaired, the CRAWFORD would search from Two Harbors south and swing up the Keweenaw.

At 8:30 a.m., December 14, the station crew began clearing ice away from the boat ways, cutting a channel through the iced-in harbor to open water. Using heavy ice spuds and hand saws, the crew cut away and hoisted out more than 10 tons of block ice. In spots, it was four feet thick! At 3:15 p.m. the lifeboat was launched. By the time it was dark a channel 200 feet long was completed.[6]

At 4 a.m. the next day, the crew turned out in the frigid predawn darkness and completed cutting the channel. At 7:00 a.m., with a favorable east-southeast wind, the crew departed for Manitou Island. After running only six miles, they were overtaken by a south gale and a northeast sea and blizzard. The boat and the Coast Guardsmen were soon sheeted in ice. They could not continue. Even getting back to Eagle Harbor was a fight. Drift ice had nearly closed their channel and the route back to the station was difficult.

Shortly after the crew returned the gale struck in force. Boatswain Glaza advised the KAMLOOPS' agents to charter a commercial tug to make the check.

In the days that followed the Coast Guard again tried to reach the Keweenaw Point area with the lifeboat, but shifting fields of ice blocked the way. Finally, in desperation, they made a 16-mile snowshoe patrol and conducted a land search. But it was fruitless. They found nothing.

The Dominion Towing and Wrecking Company's powerful tug JAMES WHALEN searched for the steamer under a roving commission from the Canada Steamship Lines. She made several trips down the waters off Isle Royale and the Keweenaw. Aboard the tug were provisions and clothing for the steamer's crew just in case.

Captain Gehl of the tug CHAMPLAIN returned to Port Arthur on the 14th and suggested that the Isle Royale area be immediately searched. The CHAMPLAIN had been en route to the ALTADOC when she diverted to investigate the possibility that the KAMLOOPS was also on the point. In the east end of the Lake, the tug MURRAY STEWART of the Soo scouted for wreckage.

One of the most exhaustive searches was made by Captain Fader in the small steamer ISLET PRINCE. Starting December 12, he departed Port Arthur and began searching the north shore. One theory had it that the

KAMLOOPS made for this area in search of shelter. The ISLET PRINCE hoped to find her hidden away in one of the shore's lonely little bays.

When the ISLET PRINCE returned to Port Arthur on the 17th, she had covered 250 - 300 miles of coastline from Thunder Bay east to the Slate Islands. She hadn't found a clue.

During the absence of the ISLET PRINCE, ice had formed in Thunder Bay and the ice-breaking tug STRATHMORE had to break a path for her into the dock.

Captain Fader had questioned all the lightkeepers along the search route. The Slate Island keeper didn't see any vessels in his area. The keeper at Battle Island reported one vessel had been off his station for two days and nights, but Fader thought this was probably the MARTIAN. The Lamb Island keeper had a possible clue. He had seen a lone steamer near the station for a full day and night, but he couldn't identify it.

Until the close of navigation, other commercial steamers kept a lookout for wreckage but found nothing. Even the efforts of a searching airplane were in vain. The KAMLOOPS had completely disappeared!

On May 26, 1928, the missing KAMLOOPS again jumped into the news. David Lind, an Isle Royale fisherman, discovered two bodies and a beach filled with wreckage on the west shore of the island.

The Coast Guard cutter CRAWFORD was immediately ordered to investigate the report.

The order caught the cutter at a rather inopportune time. She was high and dry in the Duluth Marine Iron and Shipbuilding Company dry dock in Duluth. The two propellers damaged in the ALTADOC rescue were just now being repaired and a new reverse gear was scheduled to be installed.

The message ordering her to Isle Royale was received at 9 a.m. In less than two hours the dry dock had flooded down and the CRAWFORD was underway. After a brief stop at Two Harbors, Minnesota, she headed for Isle Royale, arriving at Amygdaloid Island at 9:30 a.m., May

27. There she picked up three fishermen, including David Lind. Towing their fishing boat behind, the cutter headed for Twelve O'Clock Point, the site of the discovery.

The CRAWFORD recovered two bodies, one on the beach and one from Green Island. Each wore a lifevest clearly marked "Kamloops." After a brief and futile search along the shore for others, the cutter delivered the remains to Port Arthur, arriving there at 5 p.m. In inquest the following day by Canadian authorities reached the verdict of death by drowning.

Captain Christianson of the CRAWFORD didn't agree with that verdict. He thought it more probable that the cause of death was the bone-chilling temperature the night of the wreck. It had reached 30 degrees below zero!

Christianson also expressed the belief that the KAMLOOPS was probably lying on a rock shelf close inshore and just off Twelve O'Clock Point, possibly within 300 feet of the unnamed bay in which the bodies were discovered.

He based his speculation on the examination of the KAMLOOP's pilothouse roof which had washed upon the nearby beach. The roof was cut off as if by a knife, suggesting that the spring ice action was responsible for the shearing. This suggests that the wreck had been in water shallow enough for the ice to reach it.

High on the beach were the broken remains of the KAMLOOPS' lifeboats. One of the bodies was recovered just a few yards from it. This evidence suggested to the CRAWFORD's captain that the steamer's crew had time to launch at least one boat and had made it nearly to shore before being smashed by the seas. Perhaps the KAMLOOPS itself had struck the jagged reef extending from Twelve O'Clock Point and drifted off to sink in water just off the point.

Captain Martin Christianson of the small steamer WINYAH also viewed the wreckage and offered his opinion. The field of wreckage ran for a city block between Green and Hawk Islands. Among the field were four life buoys marked "Kamloops," half a lifeboat, five or six pair of oars, a cabin roof, and all kinds of small items including candy, toothpaste, medicine and food. It must have been a real bonanza for the island's fishermen.

In early June, Christianson of the WINYAH reported the discovery of six more bodies, less than a block from the location of the first two in May. They were badly decomposed, but he believed that one might have been a woman. There was some speculation that wolves might have taken their toll.

Some thought that the crew may have reached shore alive and died from the terrible cold. This theory received support when papers that had never touched water were removed from the pockets of several bodies. However, the Canadian Steamship Lines head office released a statement saying all the speculation was false and that the crew had drowned while attempting to reach shore. The bodies in question were actually discovered earlier in the spring by an old Indian. Reportedly he found them in a rough lean-to. One, the mate was dressed in his storm clothes and sitting on a log as if he were still alive. His right hand was tightly clenched around a single life-saver. All were frozen stiff.

Canada Steamship Lines sent the tug CHAMPLAIN to the island, complete with a search party and an under-taker. Her job was a gristly one, to recover the bodies and look for more.

All told, nine bodies were recovered, all from the same area.[7] Aside from these silent witnesses, no additional clues to the KAMLOOPS' fate were found.

The questions continued. Did she hit the "high mass of rock" on the east side of Isle Royale as suggested by Captain Simpson of the QUEDOC? If so, how did the lifeboats, bodies and wreckage reach the west side?

Did the KAMLOOPS manage to avoid the rocks and make it past Passage Island only to suffer disabling damage that would cause her to drift to her death in the waters off Twelve O'Clock Point?

The question of "what happened to the KAMLOOPS?" remained unanswered for 50 years.

As in the case of the MANISTEE and HENRY B. SMITH, a note in a bottle was eventually found.[8] A trapper discovered the bottle at the mouth of the Agawa River on the Canadian shore a year after the disappearance. He turned the message over to Captain H.J. Brian, brother of the KAMLOOPS' captain. As the note was supposedly signed by the KAMLOOPS' stewardess, Captain Brian had it authenticated by her parents. It was nearly illegible, but they thought it was from their missing daughter.

The note supposedly requested that the contents not be made public until certain conditions were met. This condition might have been an attempt to camouflage the trapper's desire for cash. He wanted to sell the note and saw no reason to reveal its contents prematurely. Whether he did sell it wasn't reported in the newspapers and the entire affair remained unresolved.

The contents of the note were never publicly revealed. It would be difficult to judge definitively at this late date the note's authenticity, but if experience is a valid guide, it was probably a hoax.

It is interesting to speculate on the KAMLOOPS fate. And for years the last voyage was recreated in the minds of the searchers, again and again.

Captain Simpson's report states that the KAMLOOPS was behind him when he narrowly avoided striking the tip of Isle Royale. Probably the "mass of rocks" he avoided was South Government Island on the east side of Blake's Point.[9] There is deep water at the island's base and a vessel could approach closely and still turn away to starboard and safety. Continuing on the starboard course, Captain Simpson would have soon cleared Blake Point and picked up Passage Island. From there he would have swung back on a course for Fort William.

As no wreckage was found near the northern tip of the island by any of the searching craft, there is no reason to assume that the KAMLOOPS did not complete the turn to safety, although the maneuver was conducted out of sight of the QUEDOC.

Captain Simpson may not have known exactly where he was that storm-driven night, but when confronted with the rocks ahead he instinctively turned to starboard and safety. Captain Brian was as skilled a sailor as

Captain Simpson and would have done the same. Both men recognized the rocks as Isle Royale.

It is unlikely that the rocks looming out of the fog were part of Passage Island, as a turn to starboard there would have taken both vessels into the treacherous reefs of Gull Islands several miles to the north. A ring of reefs also extends from the island on the east side, making a close approach difficult if not impossible.

Although there are no confirmed sightings of the KAMLOOPS on the west side of Isle Royale, there was a newspaper report that the steamer WINNIPEG sighted her on the night of December 6 during the height of the gale seeking shelter off Point Porphyry on the north shore. There is also the Lamb Island Lightkeeper's report of the unidentified steamer off his station. It is certainly possible that either vessel might have been the KAMLOOPS. If so, she certainly reached the west side of the island. But if the KAMLOOPS was on the west side, why did she fail to reach Fort William?

Somewhere along the voyage she must have sustained heavy damage. The fact that the KAMLOOPS was nearly new seems to rule out engine failure. However, if she lost her stack the engine would have effectively been rendered useless. Without the stack, there would have been no draft.

Perhaps the strain of making an extreme turn to starboard damaged her rudder. Perhaps she ran too close to the rocks and struck a reef with either propeller or rudder. Being forced into the trough of the waves might have shifted her cargo and given her a dangerous list and it's possible she was proceeding with damage suffered in an earlier incident.

In any case she probably struggled past Blake Point and on toward safety at Fort William. At this point her situation was desperate. About midway between Isle Royale and Thunder Bay the damaged part probably gave way completely and the KAMLOOPS was thrown to the mercy of the gale. Driven by northwest winds and seas, the dead hulk of the steamer drifted down on the inland's forbidding west coast.

At this point two events could have occurred. She could have foundered offshore or struck a reef (island) off Isle Royale's coast. In either case, the crew was aware of the situation, abandoned the KAMLOOPS and tried to reach safety.

Whether they managed to bring their lifeboat through the massive surf and make a successful landing only to freeze to death, or wrecked the lifeboat offshore and drowned is academic. In either instance the end result was fatal.

If the KAMLOOPS foundered offshore she would be in deep water. If she struck a reef or island, later to slip off, it was thought she could be in fairly shallow water, within the extreme limits of working depth for a scuba diver. Christianson's observation about the sheared cabin roof supports the latter possibility. Since most of the cargo wreckage and bodies were discovered in the Twelve O'Clock Point area, the region offshore could be where the KAMLOOPS is. More specifically, the hull should be somewhat north of the point and close inshore. The speculation was endless.

The KAMLOOPS early in her career.

Dossin Great Lakes Institute

On August 21, 1977, at least part of the KAMLOOPS mystery was solved. The hull of the vessel was discovered off Twelve O'Clock Point. Resting on her starboard side at the base of a steep underwater slope, her stern rail (port side) is in 175 feet and bow (starboard) is in approximately 260 feet. Her pilothouse is sheared off. Her holds have opened and a quantity of cargo spilled beneath her.[10]

Diving the wreck has proved dangerous. In August, 1979, a Canadian diver was killed on her. At the extreme depth of the wreck, the wisdom of diving her on scuba (air) is at best questionable!

FOOTNOTES

1. Much of this chapter also appears in "Went Missing," by Frederick Stonehouse.

2. The term "tramp" does not reflect on the seaworthiness of quality of the vessel. Rather, it refers to the irregular routes, schedules and cargos of the vessel.

3. The Canadian "Shipping, Casualties, Missing Vessel" report only lists a total crew of twenty.

4. Another account, published in the Annual Report of the Lake Carriers' Association, stated it was "a high dark mass" that the lookout saw. This difference could be important as it could indicate just where the two vessels came onto Isle Royale. The description "a mass of rocks" is from a published interview with the QUEDOC's captain.

5. This technique was used in the ALTADOC rescue.

6. From personal experience I can vouch for the fact that cutting through ice is a hellish task. I once spent the better part of a day cutting a three-foot by forty-foot channel around a tugboat and never worked so hard in my life.

7. Later in the year some additional floaters were found on the northern shore.

8. The MANISTEE, a 184 foot steamer went missing off the Keweenaw with all hands on November 15, 1883. The 525 foot steel steamer HENRY B. SMITH went missing with all hands off Marquette on November 9 - 10, 1913.

9. It certainly is conceivable that it may also have been one of the string of islands running southwest from South Government.

10. There was a report that a Canadian hard-hat diver found her in 1959, but it was never proven.

BIBLIOGRAPHY

"ANNUAL REPORT OF THE LAKE CARRIERS ASSOCIATION," 1927.
Boyer, Dwight. "Great Stories of the Great Lakes." New York: Dodd, Mead and Company, 1966.
Chynoweth Collection. Michigan Technological University Archives, Houghton, Michigan.
Correspondence between Canadian Department of Marine and Fisheries and Commandant, U.S. Coast Guard, dated June 11, June 15, 1928.
Correspondence with Canada Steamship Lines, November 22, 1976.
Correspondence with Isle Royale National Park, September 28, 1978.
Correspondence with the National Archives, April 5, 1976.
Correspondence with the Public Archives of Canada, November 17, 1976.
Correspondence with Thomas Appleton, Canadian Coast Guard Historian, November 23, 1976.
"DAILY MINING JOURNAL" (Marquette, Michigan). December 7, 8, 10, 15, 17, 19, 22, 24, 1927.
"DETROIT TIMES." January 21, 22, 1929.
"EVENING NEWS" (Sault Ste. Marie, Michigan). January 22, 1929.
Log of the Eagle Harbor Coast Guard Station, dated December 8 - 16, 1928.
Log of the U.S. Coast Guard cutter CRAWFORD, December 15 - 26, 1927, May 26 - 28, 1928.
Memorandum from the Public Archives of Canada, dated February 10, 1975.
Michigan Department of Natural Resources. Inventory of Shipwrecks within Michigan Coastal Waters (xeroxed).
"MILWAUKEE SENTINEL." August 8, 1979.
"MINING GAZETTE" (Houghton, Michigan). December 14, 15, 16, 17, 18, 21, 22, 24, 25, 1927; May 27, 28, 29, June 1, 2, 6, 7, 23, 1928.
"NEWS TRIBUNE" (Duluth, Minnesota). December 14, 15, 16, 17, 18, 19, 23, 27, 1927; May 27, 28, 29, 31, 1928.
"NOR'EASTER." September - October, 1977.
Oikarinen, Peter. "ISLAND FOLK." Houghton, Michigan: Isle Royale Natural History Association, 1979.
Queen's University at Kingston, Douglas Library, Canada Steamship Records.
Registrar of Shipping Wr. 1(e) Form for steamer KAMLOOPS, dated February 15, 1928.

"SUPERIOR TELEGRAM." October 4, 1977.

"TIMES JOURNAL" (Fort William). December 10, 12, 13, 14, 15, 16, 19, 20, 22, 24, 1927.

Transcript of Register, steamer KAMLOOPS.

Williams, W.R. "Shipwrecks at Isle Royale." "INLAND SEAS," winter, 1956,

Wolff, Julius F. "A Hundred Years of the Coast Guard on Lake Superior." "INLAND SEAS," spring, 1976.

.... "Shipwrecks in Lake Superior." "TELESCOPE," June, 1956.

.... "They Sailed Away on Superior." "INLAND SEAS," winter, 1973.

STRANDED SASKATOON

Just the spring following the KAMLOOPS disaster, another Canadian Steamship Lines vessel met trouble at Isle Royale, although in this case with a far happier ending.

The 250 foot, 2,412 ton SASKATOON, with a cargo of 120,000 bushels of grain, was downbound from Fort William for Montreal on May 10, 1928 when she ran hard up on a rocky shelf of Rock of Ages Reef. The SASKATOON had run south from Fort William rather than east past Passage Island, because a stop at Hubbell, Michigan to load a deck cargo of copper ingots was planned. Hubbell, located on the Portage Lake Ship Canal through the Keweenaw Peninsula, served as a major shipping point for copper from the rich Keweenaw mines.

The SASKATOON's trip began normally enough. After clearing Thunder Bay she turned southwestward, intending to cut Rock of Ages closely before swinging southeasterly for Portage Upper Entry.

Although the weather was slightly hazy, tending to blur the distinction between land and water, visibility was judged to be about six miles. Because ice was still floating in the water, the log was hauled in to prevent damage as soon as the steamer turned clear of Thunder Bay. Distances run would now have to be estimated, rather than exactly recorded.

When the SASKATOON reached Rock of Ages Light and tried to determine her position, she used a four point bearing taken from the light. While the time between observations could be accurately measured, without the log the distance could not. Thus the steamer thought she knew where she was, but was not certain.

As the SASKATOON closed on the reef, all was

115

normal. The master, Captain Irish, was on the bridge handling the navigation, while the Second Officer was casually standing in the background. Although performing no duties, the Second Officer did notice that the vessel was well steered and on course. The normal lookout was kept with the watchman on the foredeck. The wind was fresh from the northwest with only a small sea running.

Feeling that he had run far enough south to clear the reef, Captain Irish turned to port to make for Hubbell. Just after 9 p.m. on May 10, the SASKATOON ran hard on a rocky shelf of the Rock of Ages Reef! Quickly sounding her tanks, the Captain determined although she was taking on water, his vessel was in no immediate danger.

The next morning the steamer signaled an upbound sand dredge to help pull her off. In spite of the straining dredges towline and the steamer's own engine, the SAS-KATOON remained fast on the reef. The dredge then took the steamers mate to Port Arthur to summon aid.

In response to the mate's efforts, at 11:30 p.m. that night a Dominion Towing and Salvage Company rescue fleet was underway from Port Arthur. Consisting of the tug BRONSON, lighter EMPIRE, barge COTEAU, the small fleet was led by the venerable tug JAMES WHALEN of MONARCH fame. After lightening about half of the SASKATOON's grain cargo, the tugs were able to pull the steamer free about 6 p.m. on Saturday, May 12.

By Monday, May 11, the steamer was in Port Arthur where, after unloading the rest of her grain, she was promptly drydocked. Damages were more than originally thought. Upwards of 30 hull plates needed to be replaced. In addition, there was some damage to her bow. Although repairs were planned to take only three weeks, it was June 19 before she sailed from Port Arthur.

An official investigation by the Dominion Wreck Commissioner revealed some interesting problems, especially in showing just how the "little things" can cause a wreck.

The bearings taken to the light were made from inside the pilothouse by an obsolete hand and arm method in coordination with the ships compass. This was considered to be inaccurate. Without a log, the distance run was at best only an estimation. Therefore the bearings must be as accurate as possible to compensate.

When the SASKATOON neared Rock of Ages Reef, the Captain never ordered a "sharp" lookout by either the watchman or the mate. At the exact time of the stranding, the watchman was not at his post, but was sounding the ballast tanks. This was a critical time for the steamer since somewhere ahead there was supposed to be a stake marking the end of the reef. The Captain even stayed on the starboard side of the bridge instead of the port, a location from which a marker would have been more visible. The Commissioner felt the lack of a special effort to see the marker to be condemnable.

Without the travel log, the Captain could have asked the engineer for a count of revolutions turned, which would have given a rough guess of the distance run. However, he did not ask for this critical information.

Although the Commissioner reprimanded the Captain for an error in judgement and being too overconfident in knowing his position, in consideration for this being his first accident, he did not suspend his license.

The SASKATOON was built as hull number 20 by the Midland Shipbuilding Company of Midland, Ontario in 1927. In 1961 she was sold for partial scrapping. Her end came in 1963 when she was scutted for use as a breakwall. She was named for the city of Saskatoon, the second largest city in the province of Saskatchewan.

BIBLIOGRAPHY

"CANADIAN RAILWAY AND MARINE WORLD," June 1928.
"DAILY TIMES - JOURNAL" (Fort William). May 12, 15, 1928, June 19, 1928.
"MILLS, JOHN M. CANADIAN COASTAL AND INLAND STEAM VESSELS." Providence, Rhode Island: Steamship Historical Society of America, 1979.
"PORT ARTHUR NEWS CHRONICLE." May 12, 14, 15, 1928.
Report and Analysis, "SS SASKATOON Stranding." Public Archives of Canada, RG42, Vol. 425, file 130-511.

THE HAPPY SHIP

Ships are strange creations. Made of iron, steel and wood, they have the remarkable ability to assume the personalities and characteristics not only of their captain and crew, but also of their passengers and cargo as well.

Immigrant ships like the ALGOMA were hopeful ships. Though they were proud of being the passenger ships of the Great Lakes, they, like their passengers, were caught up in the search for a better future.

The happy ship

Michigan Technological University

There were ships like the KAMLOOPS; general cargo vessels, hard and tough ships built for a hard and tough trade. There were bulk cargo vessels; large, powerful ships like the PRINDOC and EMPEROR, nononsense ships built for a glamourless trade.

And then there were the AMERICAs. Ships with smiles on their bows.

The AMERICA was one of the smallest and one of the busiest of the Great Lakes passenger ships. She was a strange hybrid, half passenger carrier and half cargo vessel; almost a waterborne crosstown bus. Her ports of call were officially listed as Duluth, Port Arthur, Fort Williams and Isle Royale, but actually consisted of many more. A sharp blast from her whistle would bring a heavily-laden skiff out from behind a nameless island. The AMERICA's boom would swing out and several hundred pounds of lake trout would come tumbling aboard. In exchange, the now empty skiff would receive perhaps a case of cantaloupes, a crate of squawking chickens, or a barrel of flour. The process was repeated at island after island. For many, the regular visits of the AMERICA were their only contact with the outside world.

Her passengers were as varied in nature as her cargo (picks, shovels, salt, flour...even dynamite.) "There was the oil man from Texas, a full-bellied roughneck with an apoplectic eye, a short fussy wife and a half-pretty daughter, somewhat cowish. There was a little school-teacher from Atchison, Kansas, with enticing bow lips and slightly Oriental eyes under an unbecoming red hat; the two blue-eyed Oleson sisters from Minneapolis; a very raucous old lady and a more raucous old native, neither with anything to say;...a bunch of young fellows going up to work in a construction camp; a trapper stepped out of a James Oliver Curwood tale; an insurance man on his way to investigate the ruins of a summer place that had burned to the ground on a remote island, and three frisky flappers from St. Paul."[1]

The crew was also a mixed lot. From eagle-eyed Captain Edward C. Smith (known as "half Indian" Smith), proud of his trim craft, to rough deckhands, coal black stokers and immaculate waiters, they formed an interesting quilt of seagoing characters.

But the best-known of them all was the chief engineer, "...a ponderous lady's man, he always began to entertain restive females with a sheaf of snapshots showing himself in various poses with ladies of previous voyages."[2-3]

The AMERICA was described in the Booth Line advertisements as "palatial," and in many ways she was. She had a large, ornate dining saloon, a fine bar and a gambling room complete with rows of gleaming one-arm bandits. Lumberjacks and fishermen often left their season's earnings on board because of the gambling machines so thoughtfully provided by the steamer's owners.

Loading passengers at Tobin Harbor sometime prior to 1911.

Lake Superior Marine Museum

The sailors on the AMERICA weren't treated badly at all. Although they were prohibited from the bar and gambling room, they were fed like kings, receiving the same food as the passengers. Normal fare included lake trout, brook trout, whitefish, steak and ice cream. The pay, for the times, wasn't bad either. A simple deckhand averaged $30 a month.

The steamer AMERICA, official number 107367, was built in 1898 at the Wyandotte, Michigan yard of the Detroit Dry Dock Company for the Dumbar and McMillan Company of Michigan City. She was originally 164.5 feet in length, 31 feet in beam, 11 feet in depth and 486 gross tons. Originally the AMERICA was used as an excursion steamer between Chicago and Michigan City, with an occasional foray into Lakes Huron and Erie. In 1903, the AMERICA was sold to the Booth Packing Company (U.S. and Dominion Transportation Company) in whose service she began work as a local steamer from Duluth to all north shore points. In 1911, to gain greater passenger and cargo capacity, the steamer was lengthened to 182.5 feet and increased her tonnage to 937 gross tons.

As a steamer, the AMERICA had her fair share of trouble. In May, 1902, while attempting to leave Duluth harbor, she struck the south pier of the canal, damaging her bow to the extent of $2,000 in repairs. Although the bow compartment quickly flooded, the bulkhead held, keeping her afloat.

On July 19, 1904, the steamer EDWIN F. HOLMES, attempting to back away from her dock opposite the AMERICA's berth, scraped her anchor across the AMERICA's upperworks and tore out five cabins. Damage was estimated at $1,200. In early October, 1908, the steamer touched a reef in Tobin Harbor and damaged her rudder shoe. After being towed to Duluth by the EASTON and subsequent drydocking, she was back in business.

While trying to leave Port Arthur on July, 9, 1909, the AMERICA ran aground on Burlington Point. Although she released herself, she was later drydocked so that 40 feet of keel and 16 hull plates could be replaced. The repair bill came to $2,500 which was a considerable sum at a time when the AMERICA's fare from Duluth to Port Arthur was $6. And that included a berth and all meals!

The AMERICA before being lengthened in 1911.

Lake Superior Marine Museum

On April 10, 1910, she stranded at Victoria Light-house off Thunder Bay. Nine days later she collided with the barge FRANK L. VANCE with little effect.

As a mark of the changing times, the AMERICA received a radio, in time for the 1910 season.

In June, 1911, while attempting to enter Two Harbors in a thick Superior fog, the AMERICA lost her way and ran her bow hard against the rocky shore.

The Captain simply threw a plank from the bow to the beach and landed his passengers and mail. Then, with the aid of a tug, the steamer worked her way off the rocks. But severe damages had been suffered. The forward compartment was filled with water and a rock weighing nearly a ton had become wedged in the bow and was carried away when the ship pulled free.

The water in the forward compartment and the extra cargo combined with the rock still wedged in the bow caused the steamer to float with her bow so far down that her screw was nearly awash. Good weather finally prevailed and she was able to struggle to Superior, Wisconsin for drydocking repair. Since she was on the blocks anyway, the opportunity was taken to lengthen her by 18 feet.

Trouble again struck the AMERICA on May 5, 1914, when she ran aground in a fog about a mile northeast of Two Harbors, Minnesota. To the amazement of those aboard the stranded AMERICA, the 470-foot, 5,619-ton freighter GENERAL O.M. POE slid out of a nearby fog bank and ran aground less than 100 feet away only 10 minutes later.

The AMERICA was badly damaged and lying in a position exposed to any northeast sea. After the 42 passengers were removed by a local tug, salvage operations were begun by the steamer EASTON, the tug MAXWELL and the wrecking scow INTERSTATE. The POE was removed without undue trouble and brought to Duluth for repairs.

On May 7, with additional help from the tug MOOSE and the wrecking scow FULLER, the AMERICA was pulled free from her precarious perch. With heavy salvage pumps running constantly to keep down the water flooding in through her punctured plates, the steamer was successfully towed to Duluth and handed over to the shipyard for repairs.

The repair work wasn't cheap. The final tab stood at $4,100, but compared to the $14,200 bill for the POE, it seemed reasonable. As a result of an investigation by the U.S. Steamboat Inspection Service, Captain Smith of the AMERICA lost his license for 10 days as did the master of POE.

The AMERICA again ran aground in May, 1925, when she fetched on a reef at Scott Point near Grand Marais, Minnesota. Again, the culprit was a pea soup Superior fog. Outside assistance wasn't needed this time and she released herself without damage.

On July 21, 1927, the AMERICA rammed and sank the small tug VIOLET G. at a Port Arthur Dock.

This long litany of accidents suffered by the AMERICA was not unusual, especially when it is remembered that the vessel traveled dangerous waters from the earliest to last possible day of the season; kept closely to tight schedules regardless of the weather; made far more than an average number of dockings; and navigated frequently in waters without any aids to navigation at all. It was a wonder she didn't have more trouble!

A newspaper advertisement circa 1914 "selling" AMERICA tours.

Authors Collection

Final reckoning for the AMERICA came in predawn hours of June 7, 1928. Fred Nelson, a wheelsman on the AMERICA, gave his impression of the events that fateful morning:

"We were outbound in Washington Harbor about a half mile from the dock when the ship struck the reef. This caused a loud noise which awakened most of the crew and passengers. Those who were not up when the crash occurred came on deck when the ship's bells started ringing. Members of the crew went to cabin doors telling passengers and crew about the danger.

"The boat started sinking slowly. All five of the ship's

lifeboats were launched. Members of the crew were assigned to take charge of these boats and everyone was taken off. Captain Smith left on the last boat just before the entire ship was practically under the water.

"There was no confusion while the lifeboats were being lowered. Everyone behaved wonderfully and the six women aboard, mostly members of the crew, were not a bit excited over the crash as all saw there was no danger. All of the lifeboats reached Washington Harbor, a half mile from where the AMERICA hit the reef, without any trouble."[4]

Alerted by the AMERICA's screaming steam whistle, numerous small boats came out from Booth, Grace, Washington and Barnum Islands to help the dying ship. The only casualty in the entire wreck was a dog left tied up aft.

The actual collision with the reef occurred at 3 a.m. By 4:30 the steamer was completely underwater except for a portion of her bow that still projected above the waves.

The AMERICA stranded in the North Gap Channel.

Marquette County Historical Society

The conn had been taken over by the mate, John Wick, just five minutes before the crash. When the AMERICA plowed into the reef, Captain Smith was still on the bridge. The mate later stated that four shocks were felt as the ship hit the reef and that he ordered reversed engines and stopped the motors of the boat. A deck hand from below informed him that the boat was shipping water and that several tar barrels stored below were already underwater. At first he believed the ship would sink rapidly, but following the first gush of water she seemed to steady a bit and gave the passengers and crew plenty of time to get off.[5]

Although the mate's account doesn't mention it, an attempt to beach the AMERICA was made after she struck the reef. Losing engine power and rapidly filling with water, they fell just short of their goal.

When it was glaringly apparent that the AMERICA would sink, the Chief Engineer blew off his boilers to relieve the pressure and had his crew grease down all of the critical engine room gear. When salvaged, the AMERICA would require only a minimum of work.

A complete investigation of the loss was conducted by Captain D.T. Daniels of the U.S. Steamboat Inspection Service. Unfortunately the records of the investigation cannot be found, according to the National Archives, although the papers reported that Mate Wick was censured for careless navigation in steering a course too close to shore.

As with many shipwrecks, there were rumors of sabotage; that the AMERICA had been purposely sunk so the company could collect the insurance money. The argument ran that a new highway along Minnesota's north shore had badly cut into the AMERICA's business and the future would only show a loss of money. It was better to sink her now then to face the future! The rumors were never proved.

The small steamer WINYAH was engaged to work the route of the AMERICA for the rest of the season. However, the AMERICA's loss effectively put the Booth Line out of business.

On the beach again, the AMERICA ashore at the Devil's Track River about 1920. Notice the steamer hauling on her stern.

Lake Superior Marine Museum

The bow of the AMERICA now rests in about four feet of water with the stern in more than 80 feet. She is 200 feet off Thompson Island between Thompson Island and the main island. Easily seen from the surface, she is marked by a black buoy. The ship is tilted at a 45 degree angle and lists 30 degrees to port. Her forward deck houses are gone. As a frequent target of scuba divers, most of her "loot" has been stripped. But her holds are open as are her aft deckhouse and saloon. Her 700 HP T-3 engine still glows brightly, giving the impression that a special engineer manifests himself nightly from the underwater gloom and lovingly polishes it.

Divers can penetrate nearly every area of the wreck, although it's not entirely safe. The passageways and cabins are narrow and dark and are obstructed in some places with dangerous overhanging cables. The slightest movement inside the wreck will produce clouds of thick, vision-obscuring silt. In 1976 a diver was trapped and

The speedy AMERICA slicing through the Duluth Canal.

K.E. Thro Collection

drowned in the wreck. She seems to beckon like a Greek siren, and proves to be just as deadly.

On the starboard side, the hole that sunk the steamer can be found, complete with a steel patch ready to be clamped in place. Had the AMERICA been of double bottom rather than of a single bottom construction, it is doubtful that she would have been lost.

Captain Cornelius Flynn, a salvage diver from Duluth, visited the wreck shortly after the accident and considered her salvage to be relatively easy. After purchasing her in 1929, he set about to raise first the necessary finances and then the AMERICA. The Great Depression put an end to both.

Because the forward portion was out of the water, ice damaged it badly during the 1928/29 winter. By 1930 the vessel had skidded down the reef and was completely beneath the surface.

Another attempt was made in the middle 1960's when

a Duluth group planned to raise the steamer with compressed air and return it to that city as a tourist attraction. The lake gods frowned and their plans never materialized.

The AMERICA, her once white hull covered with a greenish-brown lake growth and her fine cabins smashed, remains but a symbol of a happy ship. . .a sunken echo of happier times.

FOOTNOTES

1. Waldron, Webb. "We Explore the Great Lakes." New York: The Century Company, 1923.

2. Ibid.

3. He must have gotten on very well with the frisky flapper from St. Paul!

4. "DULUTH NEWS TRIBUNE," June 8, 1928.

5. "DULUTH NEWS TRIBUNE," June 9, 1928.

BIBLIOGRAPHY

"ANNUAL REPORT OF THE LAKE CARRIERS ASSOCIATION," Volume 4, 1928.
Correspondence, National Archives and Records Service, April 4, 1976.
"DAILY MINING GAZETTE" (Houghton, Michigan), May 6, 1914, June 8, 10, 1928.
"GREAT LAKES PILOT." Department of Commerce, 1973.
"DULUTH HERALD." August 21, 24, 1914.
"DULUTH NEWS TRIBUNE." September 21, 28, 1905, May 6, 7, 8, 9 1914, June 8, 9, 1928.
Holden, Thom. "Above and Below: Steamer AMERICA." "NOR'-EASTER." May - June, 1978, July - August, 1978.
Larsen, Erling. "God's Country and the Ships." "SPARKS." August, 1956.
"MARQUETTE MINING JOURNAL." September 25, 1965.
"NEW YORK TIMES." June 8, 1928.
"NORDIC DIVER." July - August, 1974.
Rakestraw, Lawrence. "COMMERCIAL FISHING ON ISLE ROYALE." Isle Royale History Association, 1968.

Report of Casualty, U.S. Coast Guard. September 12, 1928.

Runge Collection, Milwaukee Public Library.

"SUPERIOR TELEGRAM" (Superior, Wisconsin). May 5, 7, 1914.

U.S. Department of Commerce, Bureau of Navigation. "Consolidated Certificate of Enrollment and License, Steamer AMERICA." Minnesota, 1927.

Waldron, Webb. "WE EXPLORE THE GREAT LAKES." New York: The Century Press, 1923.

Williams, W.R. "Shipwrecks at Isle Royale." "INLAND SEAS." Winter, 1956.

Wolff, Julius F. "Canadian Shipwrecks on Lake Superior." "INLAND SEAS," Winter, 1978.

Wolff, Julius F. "THE SHIPWRECKS OF LAKE SUPERIOR." Lake Superior Marine Museum, 1979.

ABOARD THE GOOD SHIP COX[1]

Low-lying fog softly blanketed the rocky southern end of Isle Royale. The sea was nearly flat beneath the curly-grey tendrils of cloud. This aura of unreality was heightened by the masts of a steamer moving eerily through the dense mist.

From his 11-story lighthouse, keeper John F. Soldenski stared out at the unearthly scene before him. The twin masts slowly turned until they lined up directly with the lighthouse. Soldenski frantically sounded the fog whistle, but the strange steamer held her course.

The GEORGE M. COX ready to start her last cruise.
Mariners Museum

The horrified keeper watched the masts grow larger with each passing moment. Suddenly the unknown steamer struck Rock of Ages Reef between the light and the buoy!

This story begins in 1901, 32 years before the steamer hit the reef. It was then that the PURITAN, official number 150898, slid down the ways of the Craig Yard at Toledo and first tasted fresh water. Her owners, the Graham and Morton Transportation Company, were proud of the new steamer. At 233 feet in length, 40 feet in beam, 26 feet in depth and 1,547 gross registered tons, she was a vessel of good size. In 1908 she was lengthened to 259 feet, increasing her tonnage to 1,792. Until 1918, she made regular runs from Chicago to Benton Harbor and St. Joseph with an occasional foray to Mackinac Island. All the while she carried happy vacationers in luxury and comfort.

Sold to the Michigan Transit Company in 1918, the PURITAN was quickly taken over by the United States Navy during World War I for services as a troop transport and training ship.[2]

1919 found her back in regular passenger services under the colors of the Chicago, Racine and Milwaukee Line. In 1933 the veteran vessel was purchased by George M. Cox, a New Orleans lumber and shipping magnate. His intention was to operate cruises between Chicago and Fort Williams under the ship's new name, GEORGE M. COX.[3]

Cox formed a new company, the Isle Royale Transit Company, and listed the COX and the steamer ISLE ROYALE as his principal assets. With the Century of Progress Exposition scheduled to open in Chicago, Cox believed his ship would have no trouble finding passengers.[4]

The COX was also intended to be used for weekend cruises from Chicago to Mackinac Island and points between. The larger ISLE ROYALE (310 feet) would be used for the regular Chicago-Isle Royale passenger runs.

The ISLE ROYALE was far more elaborate than the COX. She had accomodations for 400 passengers, an 80 by 30 foot range floor, a large lounge and a sports deck. A "first class" floor show with 10 women led by Fifi D'Orsay of film and vaudeville fame and a dance band

The COX on the rocks.

Lake Superior Marine Museum

were also featured.

Before leaving Chicago on her first trip, the COX was given a completely new look to include a coat of sparkling white paint for her hull and a sheen of black for her stack.[5] New staterooms, cabins and other accommodations were also built on her upper deck.

She left Chicago almost empty on her inaugural trip intending to pick up a full capacity of 250 passengers at Thunder Bay (Fort William-Port Arthur). The 18 passengers that were already aboard were friends of the owner enjoying a "free ride." Her trip up Lake Superior and through the Keweenaw waterway was totally uneventful. But things were about to liven up.

At approximately 2 p.m., May 28, 1933, the COX left Houghton, Michigan and proceeded to the western end of the waterway. There she cranked-up her engines and set her course for Rock of Ages Light, where she would turn to starboard for the run to Fort William. Her captain was George Johnson, a veteran lake skipper from Traverse City. Johnson turned the watch over to the First Mate and went below. The steamer sped on at 17 knots over the flat gently undulating lake surface through patchy fog until approximately 6:30 in the evening. Then it happened.

Some of the guests had just been seated for the evening meal when the steamer struck the reef with a fearful crash. The COX's orchestra was just beginning to play when the world seemed to collapse all around them. Fine crystal shattered to the deck. Furniture slid down the compartment and crashed against the bulkhead. Steaming trays of food flew into the air as stewards were unceremoniously thrown to the deck. The stunned passengers picked themselves up and ran outside to learn of their plight.

The ship's nurse, 23-year old Adeline Keeling, described her experience:

"There was one heavy thud, followed by a series of crashes. The passengers were at dinner at the time. . .I saw a heavy buffet table slide across the floor and crash into tables and a partition. I was in my stateroom and was thrown against a door and stunned. The stewardess, Beatrice Cole, helped me to my feet and was herself knocked down in the second crash. There was no panic, but the steamer listed heavily to port and the passengers and crew rushed to starboard. It was impossible to lower the starboard boats because of the list of the vessel, but the port boats were lowered and ferried us all to the Lighthouse."[6]

The COX had 110 feet of her white bow high in the air, like the canine tooth of a giant beast. Her aft was awash and she was listing 40 degrees to port. The force of the crash ripped the engines from their moorings. The ship's wireless immediately began to tap out an SOS.

The stern half of the COX still high on Rock of Ages Reef after the bow broke off and sank.

Archives, Michigan Department of State

At the Coast Guard dock in Two Harbors, Minnesota, the cutter CRAWFORD was engaged in the normal Saturday routine. Following are excerpts from the CRAWFORD's log:

Midnight to 9 A.M.

Vessel moved to dock at Two Harbors, Minnesota.

6:00 call all hands. Crew carried out morning routine duties. Inspected magazine and powder samples condition, dry and normal. Warmed up main engine. 8:00 liberty party returned on time.

9:00 A.M. to 4:00 P.M.

Vessel moored as before. Crew engaged in various duties about the vessel. . .11:20, inspection of ship and bedding, tested Flood Cock. 1:00 granted liberty to watch until 9:00 A.M. tomorrow.

4:00 P.M. to 8:00 P.M.

6:00 received an intercepted message[7] from S.S. MORRIS TREMAINE via Port Arthur, Ontario addressed to Coast Guard Station at Portage, Michigan, stating that steamer GEORGE M. COX was on rocks in the vicinity of Rock of Ages Light and in need of immediate assistance. Passengers and crew were now abandoning ship. . .6:30 underway, proceeding to render assistance. 6:40, Two Harbors Light abeam. . .450 R.P.M. best possible speed.

8:00 P.M. to Midnight

8:20, Split Rock Light abeam. . .Keeping in constant radio with S.S. MORRIS TREMAINE throughout watch of conditions of GEORGE M. COX. Was informed by master of MORRIS TREMAINE that he would remain in the vicinity of COX until the arrival of CRAWFORD and that it was too foggy to proceed to Port Arthur, Ontario. 1:00, Officer in Charge instructed and authorized Engineer Officer to put additional weight on the governors to enable us to increase revolutions from 450 to 475 R.P.M. . . .

Midnight to 4:00 A.M. Sunday, May 28

Vessel underway as before, partly clear to dense fog, light N.E. airs. On course. . .proceeding at best possible speed, 475 R.P.M. with caution in view of dense fog with double lookout on bow. No attempt was made to reduce speed during the watch due to lives being at stake on the GEORGE M. COX.

4:00 A.M. to 8:00 A.M.

. . .standing towards Rock of Ages Light at 475 R.P.M. Vessel running on bearing of radio direction finder, there being magnetic attraction in this vicinity. It was not advisable to rely on compass course the last 15 miles. 5:10, picked up Rock of Ages fog signal dead ahead, reduced to half speed. 5:20, about a mile from light, reduced to slow speed. 5:30, Rock of Ages Light 300 feet ahead, stopped. 5:35, anchored in 3 fathoms of water. . .

The U.S. Coast Guard Cutter CRAWFORD. She sped to the rescue of the COX's survivors.

U.S. Coast Guard

As the CRAWFORD raced to the scene, the drama of the COX continued. The message the CRAWFORD had intercepted was ultimately delivered to the correct address, resulting in the hurried 6:10 departure of the Portage Station Lifeboat for the wreck. Arriving at the COX 2:15, it discovered that the passengers and crew had already been safely transferred to the Lighthouse. The transfer was accomplished by the COX's own boats with assistance from the lightkeeper who, after indirectly witnessing the crash, took the station motor lifeboat out to investigate. All told, the lightkeeper and the COX's crew removed 120 people (18 passengers and 102 crew) from the wreck. It was the largest mass rescue in Lake Superior history. The survivors huddléd in the shelter of the lighthouse throughout the cold night. The lighthouse was too small to accommodate everyone inside so they took turns inside warming themselves. Kettles of coffee were made and there's little doubt that the unexpected guests severely depleted the lighthouse's food stock.

At 4:30 a.m. the Portage Lifeboat transported 43 persons from the Light to the Washington Harbor Hotel. Returning to the Light tower, the boat, at the request of the master of the COX, and with assistance from the newly arrived Grand Marais (Minnesota lifeboat), salvaged baggage from the stranded steamer.

At 6:30, the shift of passengers, crew and baggage from the Light tower to the newly arrived CRAWFORD began. By 7:50 the last of the bedraggled survivors was brought aboard. The CRAWFORD then made a short trip to Washington Harbor to embark the passengers previously delivered there by the Portage Lifeboat. At 9:45 the CRAWFORD departed for Houghton.

Although no one was killed in the wreck, three crewmen were injured and they, with Mr. Cox and nurse Keeling, were removed to Port Arthur by the freighter MORRIS TREMAINE. The COX was a total loss of $150,000 (and had only been insured for $100,000).

In the official Report of Loss, Captain Johnson does offer a clue to the cause of the COX striking the reef. He stated, rather cryptically, that he took the steps of having "reduced to moderate speed and changing course from NW to West after sound of siren of Rock of Ages Light becoming more distinct." This explained the turning maneuver seen by the lightkeeper. Since dense fog does tend to distort sounds, the error in turning towards rather than away from the light can also be explained.

The official inquiry conducted at Houghton produced some remarkable testimony. The first mate, who had the watch from leaving Portage Entry to the actual point of impact, was accused by the Captain of not steering the given course of NW½N. Although the mate violently denied the accusation, testimony by other crewmen corroborated the Captain's charges.

Additional testimony charged the mate with deserting his post after colliding with the reef. In fact, he was seen rowing away from the COX with only one woman passenger! The Captain, seeing the mate's light load, ordered his return to the ship. The mate again denied the charges, saying that he'd stayed at his post until the very end and had assisted in launching several lifeboats before finally leaving himself. The second time he left he filled his boat with not one woman passenger but 17!

Under heavy questioning the mate broke down and cried. After slamming his fist on the table he screamed that he was being "framed by a bunch of crooks." He later engaged in a bout of fisticuffs with Captain Gilbert, Vice President and Marine Superintendent of the line, when they met in a hotel lobby.

The PURITIAN at Holland, Michigan. As the GEORGE M. COX she wrecked on Rock of Ages Reef in 1933.

The mate's previous record was not exactly a shining one. As the first mate of the steamer KIOWA, he was involved in one of the least honorable chapters of Lake

Superior maritime history. The KIOWA had gone aground off AuSable point in 1929 during a severe blizzard. Fearing the ship was about to break up, the captain led the way off her while brandishing a gun. Since the captain drowned in the storm, no punitive measures were taken against him; however, the mate lost his license for 90 days.

Although it has never been independently confirmed or placed in the official record, there is a revealing tale relating to the general state of sobriety aboard the COX. Reportedly, when she locked through the Soo, she had trouble getting into the lock. During the course of the operation, one of the crew related to a dockworker that everyone aboard was drunk and that he was leaving when she reached Houghton. If the crewman actually did jump ship, it was certainly a wise precaution showing excellent judgement.

When all the shouting, squabbling and backstabbing was finished, the entire affair is best summarized by the Rock of Ages lightkeeper's terse entry in his log for the 29th of May: "Cleaning up the mess which was made."

While the COX was on the rocks, salvage efforts, both official and unofficial, were made. The Thunder Bay tug STRATHMORE with the barge STRATHBUOY removed all moveable equipment and personal belongings of the passengers and crew, including two brand new 1933 automobiles owned by George M. Cox.

Local fishermen continually boarded the COX and stripped her of anything of value. The COX was so badly damaged by the stranding that recovery of the vessel was never considered.

During an October gale, the remains of the shattered steamer broke in two and slipped off the reef. Her bow is presently under four feet of water. She is located ¾ of a mile, 220 degrees from Rock of Ages Light. The stern is southwest of the bow in 60 - 100 feet. Unlike the AMERICA, no portion of the vessel is marked.

The COX is a fascinating experience for a diver. The bow has been nearly flattened by the years spent in sea and ice. The chain locker is relatively intact and contains an undetermined amount of anchor chain. The anchor is still attached and located just a short distance away.

Huge hull plates litter the reef, bearing silent witness to the awesome power of Superior storms and the crushing force of the ice. Other portions of the steamer, including her mammoth boilers and propeller, can be found further down the reef.

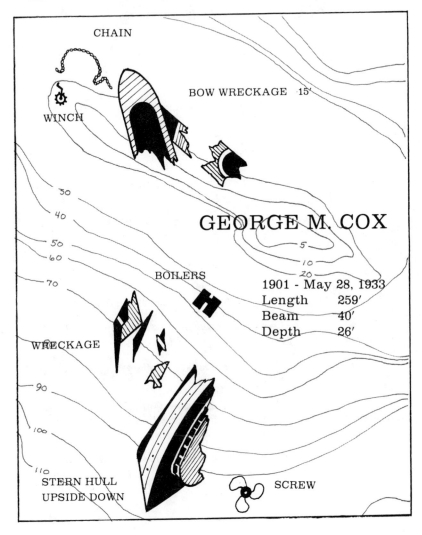

CHAIN

BOW WRECKAGE 15'

WINCH

30

40

GEORGE M. COX

50

60

70

5

10

20

BOILERS

1901 - May 28, 1933
Length   259'
Beam   40'
Depth   26'

WRECKAGE

90

100

110

STERN HULL
UPSIDE DOWN

SCREW

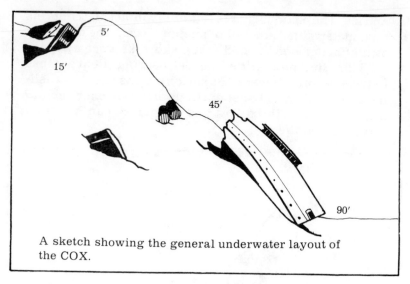

A sketch showing the general underwater layout of the COX.

FOOTNOTES

1. From an anonymous sea chanty whose language prevents its being reprinted here!

2. The Annual Report of the Lake Carriers' Association for 1933 gives a little different history, claiming she was used in the North and Baltic Seas as a mine layer.

3. Vanity knows no bounds!

4. Purchased with the PURITAN was the steamer MANITOU, which was renamed the ISLE ROYALE. After the COX disaster, the ISLE ROYALE had a particularly bad season and was moored at Manistee until 1936, when she was scrapped.

5. A poet might comment on the inescapable symbolism of the white for her past and the black for her future, but I shall not.

6. Rock of Ages Light first went into operation on October 22, 1908. Located off the western end of Isle Royale, the light shines from atop a 117-foot brick tower.

7. The actual text of the intercepted message read "GEORGE M. COX on rocks of Rock of Ages near lighthouse in bad shape." Data concerning the abandonment was received via radio communication from the CRAWFORD to the MORRIS TREMAINE.

BIBLIOGRAPHY

"ANNUAL REPORT OF THE LAKE CARRIERS' ASSOCIATION," 1933.

Brown, W. Russell. *"Ships at Port Arthur and Fort William." "INLAND SEAS."* October, 1945.

Correspondence, National Archives and Records Service, September 12, 27; October 1, 1973.

Correspondence, U.S. Coast Guard, concerning wreck of GEORGE M. COX, June 3, 10, 13, 16, 20, 27; July 28; October 16, 1933.

"DAILY MINING GAZETTE" (Houghton). May 28, 29, 30, June 1, 9, 17, 1933.

"DULUTH NEWS TRIBUNE," July 25, 1976.

"FORT WILLIAM DAILY TIMES JOURNAL," May 29, 30, 31, June 2, 1933.

Frederickson, A.C. *"SHIPS AND SHIPWRECKS IN DOOR COUNTY; VOL II."* Sturgeon Bay, Wisconsin: Door County Publishing Co., 1963.

"Journal of the Light Station at Rock of Ages." May 1933.

"Log of the Coast Guard Patrol Boat CRAWFORD." May 1933.

"NEW YORK TIMES." May 28, 29, 1933.

"Official Dispatches, U.S. Coast Guard", May 28, June 20, July 19, 1933.

"Report of Casualty, GEORGE M. COX," July 20, 1933.

U.S. Department of Commerce, Bureau of Navigation." *"Consolidated Certificate of Enrollment and License, Steamer GEORGE M. COX,"* 1932.

Vander Linden, Rev. Peter, ed. *"GREAT LAKES SHIPS WE REMEMBER."* Cleveland: Freshwater Press, 1979.

Williams. W.R. *"Shipwrecks at Isle Royale." "INLAND SEAS,"* winter, 1956.

Wolff, Julius F. *"A Lake Superior Lifesaver Reminisces." "INLAND SEAS,"* summer, 1968.

Wolff, Julius F. *"Shipwrecks in Lake Superior." "TELESCOPE,"* June, 1956.

Wright, Dr. Richard J. *"Inventory of Shipwrecks Within Michigan Coastal Waters."* Grant study funded by the Michigan Department of Natural Resouces and Northwest Ohio-Great Lakes Research Center.

A COLLISION AT SEA
CAN RUIN YOUR WHOLE DAY!

The PRINDOC before sinking off Passage Island.

Great Lakes Historical Society

Another of Isle Royale's wrecks occurred on June 1, 1943, when the Patterson Line steamer 256 foot PRINDOC was rammed in the fog and sunk by the Canada Steamship Lines package freighter BATTLEFORD. The PRINDOC, under Captain Smysell, was downbound from Thunder Bay with cargo of grain and had reached the western approaches of Passage Island, when the 246 foot Canada Steamship Lines BATTLEFORD loomed out of the gray vapor and struck the ship a mortal blow. With the steamer listing badly, the 22 crewmen of the PRINDOC abandoned ship and were immediately picked up by the BATTLE-

FORD. Within minutes, the PRINDOC sank in 580 feet of cold Superior water.

The PRINDOC was built in 1901 as the GILCHRIST by the West Bay City Ship Building Company of West Bay City, Michigan. She worked under the flag of the Gilchrist Transportation Company until 1913, when she was sold to the Interlake Steam Ship Company and renamed the LEPUS. The Patterson Lines purchased her in June of 1926 and renamed her. At 3,871 tons, 356 feet in length, 50 feet in beam and 28 feet in depth, the PRINDOC was one of the smaller lake freighters.

But small or large, a collision at sea did ruin her whole day!

BIBLIOGRAPHY

Mills, John M. "CANADIAN COASTAL AND INLAND STEAM VESSELS 1809 - 1930." Providence, Rhode Island: Steamship Historical Society of America, 1979.

"NEW YORK TIMES," June 2, 1943.

Williams, W.R. "Shipwrecks at Isle Royale," "INLAND SEAS." Spring, 1956.

Wolff, Julius F. "Before the Days of Radar: Ship Collisions on Lake Superior," "INLAND SEAS." Summer 1969.

ONE 'HECK OF A WRECK'

There are wrecks and there are wrecks. Some, when explored underwater, are nothing more than an area littered with broken planks, shattered beams and iron hull plates. They are almost reminiscent of topside garbage dumps.

There are also wrecks like the AMERICA. Intact, relatively shallow and easy to locate and explore. Then there are the EMPERORs: ships that died in dreadful agony and seem to retain an aura of their death.

With her stern in 150 feet, awning open hatches, shattered bow and the bodies of some of the crew still rumored to be entombed in the stern, she is "one heck of a wreck."

The steamer EMPEROR, official number 126654, was built in 1911 at the Collingwood, Ontario yard of the Collingwood Ship Building Company. Registered in March, 1911, at Midland, Ontario, her original owner was the Inland Lines Ltd., James Playfield, General Manager. On May 25, 1916, the steel steamer was purchased by the Canada Steamship Lines of Montreal.

She wasn't one of the largest of the bulk carriers, but at 7,031 gross tons she was respectable. Overall, the EMPEROR was 525 feet in length, 56 feet in beam and 31 feet in depth. Her 1,500 horsepower, triple-expansion engine could push her at a slow but steady 11½ nautical miles per hour.

At the time of her launching, the EMPEROR was the largest vessel ever built in Canada and the first of the 10,000 tonners. James Playfield personally christened his new steamer. The EMPEROR was the "Pride of Canada."

It was 10:55 p.m. when the EMPEROR backed away from the Port Arthur ore dock. Her massive propeller slowly pulled the heavily laden vessel away from the pools of white thrown by the rows of dock lights. With the loud rumble of the engine as accompaniment, the silent shadows swallowed the steamer. Clear of the dock, the rudder was put hard over, and the EMPEROR, with a white mustache at her bow, charged into the dark lake. The next stop was scheduled to be Lake Erie and the harbor at Ashtabula, Ohio.

At 4:45 a.m., June 4, 1947, the EMPEROR ran hard up on Canoe Rocks, on the northwest side of Isle Royale. Within 25 minutes, the powerful ship had foundered. And she was only 3¼ miles, 281 degrees from the Blake Point Light!

An SOS sent immediately after striking brought out the U.S. Coast Guard cutter KIMBALL. The KIMBALL had routinely been at Isle Royale when it received the distress call and was able to arrive at the scene within 25 minutes.

The mighty EMPEROR, the pride of the Canadian fleet when launched in 1911.

Runge Collection,
Milwaukee Public Library

The EMPEROR, light without cargo moving through slush ice in the Soo Canal.

K.E. Thro Collection

Of 33 crewmen, the KIMBALL rescued 21, picking 10 from a lifeboat half-filled with sloshing water.[1] Four crewmen were found clinging to the keel of a second overturned lifeboat and seven were picked up off Canoe Rocks itself. The KIMBALL returned the survivors to Fort William. It is not beyond the realm of possibility that at least some of those killed were sucked under when the EMPEROR sounded. Among the 12 lost were her captain, Eldon Walkinshaw of Collingwood, a lake skipper of 42 years' experience; the first mate, James Morrey, and three women stewardesses. The steamer normally would have carried a crew of 35, but two men were left behind at Port Arthur, perhaps saving their lives.

The experience of one of the survivors, a coal passer, is worth relating. Caught in the act of climbing into his bunk when the steamer hit, he grabbed his trousers in one hand and his life jacket in the other and ran to the after deck. There he assisted in lowering two lifeboats. While lowering the second boat, the "ship gave a lunge and water came gushing over me like a waterfall." Tossed into the lake by the motion, he drifted to the overturned lifeboat and hung on until the KIMBALL arrived. From the author's own experience diving the area, it must have been a numbing wait.

How the EMPEROR came to wreck on Canoe Rocks still remains a mystery. Following the loss, a Canadian Court of Investigation met in an attempt to solve the riddle. After hearing all of the testimony, it did manage to throw some light on the puzzle.

From the time the EMPEROR left Port Arthur until midnight, the watch was held by Captain Walkinshaw. He was relieved by James Morrey, the first mate, who settled in a chair in the wheelhouse from which he had a clear view forward. Visibility was excellent. The Passage Island Light, 27 miles away, was clearly in view. The first mate was not as alert as he wanted to be, however. He had spent his off-watch hours supervising the loading of 10,429 tons of ore cargo. Lulled by the calm lake and the soothing blackness of the night, the first mate fell asleep in his chair.

In addition to the first mate's inattention, there was irregularity in the courses steered. When the vessel passed Welcome Island, a course of 138 degrees true was taken. The court believed this course was not changed until just opposite Trowbridge Island Light when a course of 098 degrees true was taken. The EMPEROR should have shifted course when abreast of Thunder Cape Light instead of running abreast of Trowbridge, three miles further. The shift should have been made at Thunder Cape Light. Shifting late steered the EMPEROR far south of her normal track and directed her right to Canoe Rocks.

Since the first mate and the wheelsman were the only ones on the bridge at the time, and because both were dead, the court's conclusions were based on conjecture.

The court decided that the loss of the EMPEROR was the result of the "wrongful act of the first mate," who "did not keep proper watch."

149

A stern quarter painting of the EMPEROR under steam.

Mariners Museum

The court also criticized the "system which prevailed which required the first mate to be in charge of loading the ship during the period when he should have been off duty, and resulted in his becoming overtired, suffering as he was from lack of sleep."

The court also stated that "James Morrey was a man of wide experience on the Great Lakes, that he was most efficient and that he had an excellent record previous to this unfortunate accident."

That the EMPEROR was a well-found and seaworthy vessel cannot be denied. William F. Craig, the Steamship Inspector for the Canadian Department of Transport, stated the ship was "one of the best equipped ships I saw this spring."

The court also recommended that a system of electric gongs be installed throughout vessels for use in such a disaster. They further ruled that sufficient lifeboat drills were not held to familiarize the crews with their stations and duties.

When all the accountants were finished counting and lawyers litigating, the EMPEROR was an insurance loss of $632,700.

Within days of her loss, a local hard hat diver was on the wreck. From the early 1950's on, the wreck has become an increasing attraction for divers.

For diver exploration, the EMPEROR is "one heck of a wreck."

Resting with a list to starboard on the side of the underwater rock slope, it presents an ungodly appearance. Although the bow is under only 35 feet of water, the slant of the slope places her stern in 150 feet. Approaching the EMPEROR, the diver is completely awed by her sheer bulk. At 525 feet overall, it's only 100 feet shorter than the liner ANDREA DORIA. Careful examination of the hull will reveal the large block letters CANADA STEAMSHIP LINES.

Still just awash the day after the wreck, the pilothouse of the EMPEROR.

K.E. Thro Collection

At the bow, with visibility near 50 feet, the diver passes over the remains of her destroyed pilothouse. With a last glance at the shimmering surface, the diver begins his descent. Swimming down her main deck, he continues over the yawling black chasms of her hatches, their covers having been blown open by air trapped inside when she sank. At the number five hatch he sees a massive break running the width of the steamer. Obviously, this is where she broke. It was either after sinking (due to the uneven support of the slope), or before, during the wreck itself. Crossing over the canyon-like gap, the diver journeys into an abyss. The eerie line of hatches continues to stretch before him like the steps of a giant ladder.

The U.S. Coast Guard Cutter KIMBALL, the rescuer of 21 of the EMPEROR's crew. The KIMBALL was decommissioned in 1968.

U.S. Coast Guard

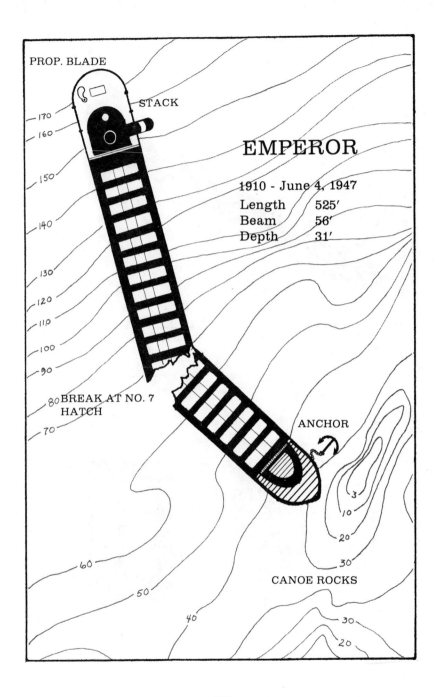

PROP. BLADE

STACK

EMPEROR

1910 - June 4, 1947

Length 525'
Beam 56'
Depth 31'

BREAK AT NO. 7
HATCH

ANCHOR

CANOE ROCKS

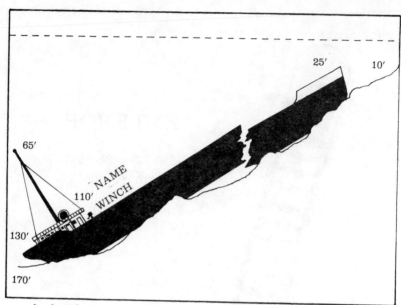

A sketch showing the present underwater layout of the
steamer EMPEROR.

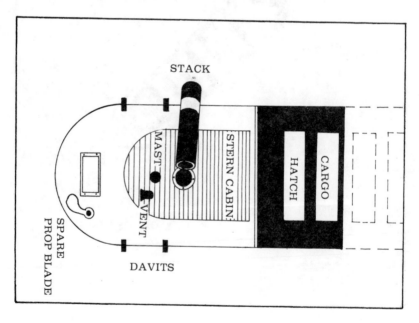

He has long since lost count of the number of hatches. His only concern now is reaching the after deck house. Visibility has dropped to 25 feet and it has become darker. A glance at his wrist thermometer indicates that the water temperature is 34 degrees!

Looming ahead, almost invisible in the surrounding gloom, is the stern cabin. Although covered with a greenish-brown slimy lake growth, it appears to be almost intact. At 150 feet in Lake Superior, exploring the hulk of a wrecked steamer, fear of the unknown and intimations of the supernatural are a common experience. It's a shadowy, phantasmal world the diver seems to be a part of and it's easy for the imagination to run wild. The ambient gloom and confusion of wreckage makes extensive examination of the wreck both fascinating and dangerous. After locating the safety lines secured to the rail, the diver begins his ascent.

Later, sitting on the deck of the dive boat, a diver feels relieved at having emerged alive from the strange world of the EMPEROR.

FOOTNOTES

1. *The water entered through an open drain plug! As a further note, the air temperature in the area hovered at 35 degrees, making it the coldest June 4th in Michigan history!*

BIBLIOGRAPHY

"ANNUAL REPORT OF THE LAKE CARRIERS ASSOCIATION," 1947.

Canadian Department of Transportation. "Transcript of Register, Steamer EMPEROR." *Midland, Ontario. March, 1911.*

Correspondence, National Archives and Records Service. July 31, November 16, December 17, 1973.

"DAILY MINING GAZETTE" (Houghton). June 4, 5, 1947; August 10, 1963.

"DAILY NEWS" (Port Arthur, Ontario). December 9, 1910.

Frimodig, Mac. Shipwrecks Off Keweenaw. Fort Wilkins Natural History Association.

"GREAT LAKES PILOT." Department of Commerce, 1973.

McWilliam, Scott. "Tragedy at Isle Royale." "DIVER." July - August, 1980.

"NEW YORK TIMES." June 5, July 3, 27, 1947.

"NOR'EASTER." September - October, 1976.

Queen's University Archives.

"Report of the Court of Investigation" into the circumstances attending the loss in the vicinity of Canoe Rocks, Lake Superior on June 4, 1947, of the S.S. EMPEROR. July 9, 1947.

"Statement of Shipping Casualties Resulting in Total Loss on the Inland Waters Excepting the St. Lawrence River Below Montreal, From 1870 up to Date." Department of Transportation, 1975.

Williams, W.R. "Shipwrecks at Isle Royale." "INLAND SEAS," winter, 1956.

Wolff, Julius F. "100 Years of Rescue, The Coast Guard on Lake Superior." "INLAND SEAS," spring, 1976.

Wolff, Julius F. "Shipwrecks in Lake Superior." "TELESCOPE." June, 1956.

Wright, Dr. Richard J. "Inventory of Shipwrecks Within Michigan Coastal Waters." Grant study funded by the Michigan Department of Natural Resources and the Northwest Ohio - Great Lakes Research Center.

HENRY STEINBRENNER

"When I saw the hatch covers blown across the deck, I knew it was all over."[1]

When the 427 foot 4,345 ton freighter HENRY STEIN-BRENNER, loaded with 6,800 tons of iron ore, pulled away from the Great Northern Railway Dock at Superior, Wisconsin, there was no reason to suspect that her trip down to Lake Erie would be anything but strictly routine. It was shortly after 5 a.m. (E.S.T.) on May 10, 1953 and 12 years since the last American freighter was lost on the lakes.[2] The feeling of complacency was further reinforced by the weather which had been simply magnificent with sunny skies and temperatures in the mid-70's. Outstanding spring weather!

Built in Port Huron, Michigan in 1901 and owned by Kinsman Transit Company, the STEINBRENNER was an old veteran of the Lakes.

Lake Superior was nearly flat, with hardly a ripple to break the surface. Later Captain Stiglin, master of the steamer, would recall that it was "smoother than a pond." The 5 a.m. and 6 a.m. forecasts called for southeast to south winds at 30 - 35 mph with occasional thunder-squalls in Superior's west half. The lake would get decidedly choppy, but nothing the STEINBRENNER couldn't handle with ease. Captain Albert Stiglin and his 30 man crew confidently began their trip.

Captain Stiglin was in command of the STEIN-BRENNER for the first time this season, but he had been with the Kinsman line for 16 of his 27 year sailing career. The 46 year old skipper had held his masters papers for seven years. For the four previous years he had been the master of the PHILLIP MINCH.

The STEINBRENNER was routinely secured for sea. Her 12 telescoping cargo hatches were closed and fastened with mulholland type clamps. There were 28 clamps on each hatch, although some of the threads were reportedly stripped. The chock and hawse pipe covers were also fitted into place. All steering and navigational equipment with the exception of her radar were in operating order. Ominiously though, tarpaulins were not fitted over the hatches. It was a decision to be later regretted.

The STEINBRENNER's trip was uneventful until about 3 p.m., May 10 when the wind freshened and the sea began to build. About 4:30 p.m. the first sea came aboard. With the weather deteriorating the crew braved the open weather deck and rechecked the hatches, chock and hawse pipe covers. Weather forecasts were still calling for south to southeast winds although now with a slight increase to 30 - 40 mph.

The 427 foot steamer HENRY STEINBRENNER.

By 5 p.m. the weather had turned bad enough that only a quarter of the crew could make it to the galley for supper. The best the cooks could rustle together was a cold meal anyway.

At 8 p.m. that night the pilothouse watch observed that a hatch leaf on the portside of the number 11 hatch had worked loose. With the decks occasionally swept by seas, the cargo hold was now open for flooding.

The third mate and three hands rigged traveling lines from the main deck lifeline cable and worked their way out from the pilothouse to the wild open deck to secure the loose hatchleaf. Again and again the men were inundated by cold grey seas sweeping the length of the steamer's deck. Without their lifelines, they would have been lost! During the struggle with the heavy steel hatch leaf, one of the deck hands was washed through the open hatch and fell 15 feet into the cargo hold. Using his safety line, the others were able to manhandle him back up and carry him to the safety of the galley/dining room. The others then returned on deck and finished securing the hatch. The clamps, however, were only hand tightened. The mate and his men were unable to return forward and were forced to shelter in the aft deckhouse. The STEINBRENNER had no passageways fore and aft through the cargo holds. The only route was over the weather deck, and with the raging gale that was suicide!

By 11 p.m. the STEINBRENNER was beleagured by a full lake storm. The east northeast wind was gusting up 80 mph and the sea continuing to build. Later, a wild-eyed survivor would claim the seas grew to over 60 feet! More accurate estimates placed their height at 20 feet plus, although a 30 footer wasn't uncommon.

About 6:30 a.m., May 11, a sea crashed through one of the forecastle deck observation room doors. Quickly, two men secured the door back in place by jamming heavy planking behind it. An hour later another sea broke through it, and again it was secured. A third sea ripped out the two inch wooden door, hinges, jam, bracing and lock intact! The seas also found entry through the port chock in the windlass room. Later one of the crew would claim that the battering of the waves was so bad, the pilothouse was shifted three feet back!

Sometime about 4:30 a.m. the hatch leaf on the number 11 hatch again worked loose. But now the sea conditions were such that it was impossible for anyone to go on deck to secure it. Instead both ballast pumps were started and suction taken on both port and starboard sides of the number 4 cargo hold. Captain Stiglin later observed, ... "solid water was pouring in over both sides of the ship. There was no way to stand on deck."

One of the deck hands who earlier assisted in securing the hatches remembered "water was pouring into number 11 hatch at the stern. Every time she rolled, the hatch would roll and the water poured in."

The midnight weather forecast was finally *beginning* to catch up with actual conditions. It predicted winds, shifting to the northeast and blowing 45 - 50 mph, with intermitant thundersqualls.

Conditions in the open lake, however, were far worse. The steamer was being pounded badly, and the seas were climbing on board and constantly covering her hatches. With the STEINBRENNER heading into the wind, the seas were sweeping aboard from both sides, swirling over and down the weather deck, around the after deckhouse to the fantail. To ride easier, the steamer had checked down her speed to about 4.8 mph. During the height of the storm, Al Augsburger, one of the oilers, remembered the steamer was actually taking water down her stack!

By 6 a.m., May 11, the pilothouse crew noticed the STEINBRENNER was becoming sluggish. An hour later they saw other hatch covers working. If the vessel was to be saved, fast action would have to be taken to secure them. Clearly the pumps were unable to handle the flooding and the vessel was slowly settling deeper and deeper.

Accordingly, the captain gave her hard left rudder and full power to bring her around to the opposite course in an attempt to give the after end of the weather deck enough shelter to allow crewmen to secure the hatches.

Hopefully this would slow the flooding and allow the overworked pumps to catch up. The maneuver did no good. The seas continued to wash over her decks with grasping malevolence . It would have been suicide to venture on deck. After 10 minutes the steamer was brought around to her original course, but only after spending several terrifying minutes caught in the deadly trough of the waves.

Shortly past 6 a.m., after she was back on her original heading, Captain Stiglin broadcast a call for help on his radio and alerted his crew to put on life jackets. Six vessels, the 650 ft. WILFRED SYKES, 682 ft. JOSEPH H. THOMPSON, 580 ft. D.M. CLEMSON, D.G. KERR, WILLIAM E. COREY, ONTADOC and HOCHELAGA heard the call and headed for the scene.

At 7:30 a.m. the three after hatch covers (10-11-12) came loose. The general alarm was immediately rung, and Captain Stiglin ran up "stop" on the pilothouse Chadburn. The engine room answered and the STEINBRENNER started to lose way. Another radio call for help was made, now giving her position as 15 miles due south of Isle Royale Light. By now the engine room had flooded. Water had already reached the grate bars and was threatening the red hot boiler.

Six minutes later, at 7:36 a.m., the abandon ship signal was blown. At the forward end of the vessel ten of the crew gathered around the liferaft on the forecastle deck. Aft, the men stood by on the boat deck and on signal attempted to launch the 20 man lifeboats. The starboard (#1) boat swung out with seven men aboard, but the men remaining were not able to launch the remaining port (#2) boat.

As a last resort, the boat was unshackled from the falls. When the STEINBRENNER suddenly sank stern first the boat floated clear, although one of the two men working inside trying to insert the boat plug was thrown out. Later two other crewmen managed to swim to the safety of the waterlogged, damaged lifeboat. The remaining crewman was slammed across the boat and fatally injured by the violence of the foundering.

Marking the Middle Island Passage is Rock Harbor Light. Built in 1855, it was the original light on the island. It was abandoned prior to 1900.

Meanwhile up forward, standing with the liferaft, Captain Stiglin clearly remembered the events. "..I saw the two lifeboats clear the ship. I know that all men were clear for I caught a brief glimpse of the two boats clear of the after deck. The nine men and I climbed on the fore-castle liferaft as the ship sank lower and lower. When the raft started to float, a wave capsized it and we lost four men, for only six climbed back on the raft."

When the raft capsized, Captain Stiglin was thrown out into the water and partially sucked under by the sinking steamer. When he finally surfaced, it was directly under the raft.

Considered by the Coast Guard as capable of carrying 15 men, the 6 ft. x 12 ft. liferaft was of metal air tank and woodframe construction. Although it kept the men figuratively above the water, it was scant protection to them. They were continually drenched by the freezing water and chilled by the racing arctic wind.

One of the survivors, Kenneth Kumm, later remembered, "I was ready to dive in and swim ashore when I saw Isle Royale. . .I was standing on the rail ready to jump when one of the guys grabbed me and said the water's too cold, you'll never make it! Then I got hit by a wave and that's what saved me, it washed me right down to the middle of the ship. I remember opening my eyes underwater. . .I guess I passed over four or five hatches. When I came up for air and started swimming I was only ten feet from the lifeboat. The ship sank right as I reached the lifeboat."

Witnesses in the lifeboat later testified that as the after deck disappeared beneath the waves, the still red hot boilers exploded from contact with the icy water and debris flew through the air. Kenneth Kumm was swimming when the boiler went off. He actually felt a flash of heat pass through the icy water!

As the no. 1 lifeboat was drifting past the stern of the STEINBRENNER, one of the men looked up and saw an assistant engineer standing at the stern of the ship just looking down at them. The observer in the lifeboat thought this was most peculiar. Evidently, some of the crew preferred to take their chances sticking with the ship rather than leaving her. The feeling was indeed prevalent that as Al Augsburger remembered it:

"What the hell good is that little boat (lifeboat) going to be if the big one goes down."

The survivors spent a cold, wet miserable four and one-half hours before finally being picked up at approximately 11 a.m.

On the liferaft Captain Stiglin later reported "we spent four hours on the raft. It bobbed up and down on the top of the high waves. Spray blew over us, drenching our clothing. Once we saw one of the lifeboats bobbing in the water. The first mate lost consciousness on the raft. He died shortly after the rescue ship showed up."

Those on the lifeboat were terribly overcrowded. Although he wasn't aboard, Kumm remembered looking at the tiny raft with others of the crew and wondering just how it could hold them all. The captain had earlier told them the raft would be their best bet!

The five men on the life raft were rescued by the JOSEPH H. THOMPSON and the seven men in the starboard lifeboat by the D.M. CLEMSON. An occupant of the starboard lifeboat, Augsburger remembered "we huddled up in the canvas sea anchor, that's what kept us alive. Another half hour and we would have been dead." He also remembered "the Coast Guard flew over, but didn't see us."

As there are no atheists in foxholes, so are there none in lifeboats. Augsburger remembered he got more religion in four hours drifting in the lifeboat than he could have received in four years in a seminary. The rescue by the CLEMSON seemed a miracle to him. "When I saw that big tin stack coming through the water, it was beautiful."

The CLEMSON missed them on the first pass, and the lifeboat came dangerously near the big steamers churning prop. It would have been ironic had the seven seamen survived their long ordeal only to find death at a rescuers hands! On the second attempt, the CLEMSON was successful and one by one the seven frozen men were hauled aboard at the end of a heavy manila line.

Aboard the waterlogged port lifeboat, Kenneth Kumm remembered all that saved him and his companion was their size and weight. Kumm thought he went from 225 pounds to 185 pounds in four hours. There was no bucket to bail the lifeboat out, but it didn't matter as the waves were washing into the boat so rapidly that the frigid water was coming in quicker than the two half frozen men would have thrown it out. After an hour, the men were numbed both physically and mentally. They didn't dare move for fear of being washed out!

The SYKES first learned of the STEINBRENNER's troubles when the first mate heard Stigln's original radio call for aid. At the time the SYKES was 35 miles distant. She and the JOSEPH H. THOMPSON arrived at the scene at the same time.

Captain George Fisher of the SYKES initially spotted the half flooded lifeboat when it pitched high on the crest of a wave. The lifeboat was pulled to the SYKES and when a Jacob's ladder was dropped, Kenneth Kumm managed to grab it with the strength of a "death grip." The SYKES crew had to haul both the ladder and the frozen Kumm aboard together. But before anyone else could follow, a swell whipped the lifeboat and the line snapped.

To make another try at saving the men, Captain Fisher brought the massive SYKES around in a full circle which served to cut down the sea. Although effective, the maneuver took almost an hour.

But to complete the rescue, the third mate, Arthur Ritter, and nine men voluntarily lowered the SYKES lifeboat and used it to bring the STEINBRENNER boat in. The sea conditions were terrible, and their action took a remarkably high degree of seamanship and a healthy dose of, in Mate Ritter's words later when praising his volunteer crew, ". . .plenty of guts. ."

The Canadian steamer ONTADOC was upbound and off Passage Island, near the north tip of Isle Royale, when she heard the STEINBRENNER call for aid. After contacting the downbound HOCHELAGA, the ONTADOC turned around and with the HOCHELAGA, headed for the STEINBRENNER. Both vessels worked their way down the east coast of Isle Royale with the ONTADOC keeping well inside the larger HOCHELAGA for protection. As late arrivals at the scene they both laid several miles off and stood by to render any help needed. Through glasses, the crews watched fascinated as the THOMPSON, CLEMSON and SYKES performed their brave rescues amid the mountainous waves. Later Captain W.A. Boult of the ONTADOC observed, "I wonder sometimes that they didn't turn over," and "those fellers really were using their heads."

Other carriers participating in the search were the IMPERIAL LEDUC, and the PATHFINDER. The Coast Guard Bouytender WOODRUSH from Duluth, as well as lifeboats from the Portage Ship Canal, Grand Marais, Minnesota and Two Harbors also searched the area. In the following days and weeks a total of ten bodies were recovered but seven remained missing.

Strangely, although advance warning had been given, some of the crew appeared on deck without their life jackets. The third mate and his three men, trapped in the aft deckhouse and unable to reach their jackets stored in the forward cabins, used jackets from the life- boats. Many of the engine room gang also arrived without lifejackets. Theirs were in their cabins on the open spar deck. As this deck was constantly swept by the seas, it was too dangerous to attempt to reach them. Nonetheless there was an element of panic as there were four jackets stored and available in the engine room "telephone booth."[3] In their haste, these were forgotten.

The panic manifested itself in other ways. Oiler Augsburger remembered one of the men on the stern had enough sense to bring some blankets, but instead of throwing them into the lifeboat, he meaninglessly stuffed them down a ship's ventilator!

Augsburger remembered there was nothing orderly about the evacuation. From his position on the stern panic stricken men were common. In fact, one rare act of orderliness nearly cost the lifeboat crew their lives. It seems one of the men was an ex-Coast Guardsman, who, as a result of his years of Coast Guard training routinely secured the lifeboat painter to the STEINBRENNER's rail. Thus when the lifeboat was lowered into the water and cast off from the falls, it was still secured to the rapidly sinking steamer! Since no one had a knife to cut the painter, it appeared the lifeboat and all aboard would be pulled under to their deaths when the steamer sank. By pure luck, the third assistant engineer, Arthur Morse, appeared on deck and released the painter. Morse, however, made no effort to jump to the lifeboat. Instead, he went down with the ship.

One of the engine room crew, Harry Johnson, kept his wits about him very well, but then he had had a great deal of experience having been torpedoed twice in the Atlantic during World War II! The engine had been stopped when the order came to abandon the steamer but before Johnson left the engine room he dropped the throttle some to allow the STEINBRENNER to "run away" from the lifeboats. It was an old trick he had learned on the north Atlantic to put as much distance as possible between the survivors and exploding boilers.

In contrast with the panic stricken aft, the forward end was calm and orderly, undoubtedly due in part at least to the steady leadership of Captain Stiglin, a man well respected by his crew. Kenneth Kumm, a forward end man, remembered there was no panic among the crew, that in the grip of the storm there was nothing that could be done and no time to do it. There was mostly pure shock at what was happening to them.

When Captain Stiglin disembarked from the THOMPSON at the Soo, his terse statement concerning the loss was that "the decks were awash and she was rolling and pitching. Three hatch covers were swept away and she filled with water." Captain Stiglin then went directly to the Objibway Hotel to confer with company lawyers. Losing a ship is always a nasty affair requiring the best of legal advice!

The crew that disembarked at the Soo were treated decidedly shoddy, being hustled about more like cattle than men. Eventually each man submitted a detailed inventory of his posessions lost when the STEINBRENNER sank. After the Coast Guard took the survivors' testimony, the company paid each man a $300 "sinking fee" but deducted the cost of new clothing required to appear before the Coast Guard Board. The company wanted the men to look their best, but didn't see why they should bear the expense. The families of the men lost, of course, received the full $300, with no deductions.

Worst of all, was the fact that many of the survivors left the STEINBRENNER without even enough money to buy a beer. The company made no effort to advance any money either! Luckily the residents of the Soo took pity on the shipwrecked mariners and stood them to all the libations needed.

The remaining survivors were disembarked at Duluth, where the treatment was decidedly better. Kumm remembered being treated to an excellent meal, by a citizen who would take no thanks and remained anonymous!

The forward liferaft from the STEINBRENNER alongside the THOMPSON.

K.E. Thro Collection

Some of the STEINBRENNER's crew were very critical of the 52 year old steamer. One of the watchmen claimed "nothing worked as it should aboard the ship. We were taking water something awful for nearly 12 hours before she went down." "For my money she just wasn't seaworthy!" He also indicated that some of the stripped clamps were indeed on the after three hatches, a point the Board of Investigation seemed to miss. Another crewman called her a "scow barge" while yet another said she was "just too old."

But yet others said the old steamer had indeed been seaworthy. There was no question she was a "bucket," but oiler Augsburger had sailed in her the year before and "been through some good blows in her."

For her part in the rescue of the two STEINBRENNER crewmen from the lifeboat, the Inland Steel Company steamer WILFRED SYKES was honored by the company officials. At that time the SYKES was the flagship of the Inland Steel fleet and the holder of most of the speed and tonnage records on the Great Lakes. Each officer and crewman was presented with a savings bond as recognition of the company's pride in the accomplishment. The company stated it was "a remarkable feat of seamanship that the SYKES was even able to launch a small boat let alone rescue any of the men adrift." The operation they said, "was extremely hazardous."

The STEINBRENNER had not had the most illustrious of careers. In 1901 she was launched prematurely at her Port Huron shipyard to avoid a dockyard fire. On December 5, 1909 she collided with the steamer HARRY A. BERWIND just past Round Island in Mud Lake, in the St. Mary's River. The BERWIND struck the STEINBRENNER amidships and tore a 25 ft. hole in her, quickly sending her to the bottom with a cargo of coal. Although her pilothouse was clear of the water and the stern cabin only half submerged, five feet of water covered the steamer's decks.

The famous Great Lakes salvor Tom Reid was given the contract to raise her after bidding her out for $35,000. As the water of Mud Lake is very turbid during the navigational season, and the shipping channels ran right past the sunken steamer, Reid waited until the season closed and the lake iced up. Then his divers could work in relatively clear water.

When the ice froze to a depth of approximately 12 inches, Reid with the tugs PROTECTOR and J.M. DIVER began operations. Chopping a hole through the ice, the divers started work. On their first dive they discovered that during the waiting interval the STEINBRENNER had started to sink deeper in the mud, making the salvage operation more complicated. After clearing the mud away from the jagged hole, the divers applied a hull patch and waited for spring. When the ice finally left they "cofferdammed" her hull and pumped her out. The salvage was completely successful and Reid turned a profit of $10,000.

In 1923 the STEINBRENNER collided with the JOHN McCARTNEY in Whitefish Bay. Combined damages totaled $15,000 in yard work. The STEINBRENNER damaged her port bow to the extent of $24,500 in October of 1941 when she rammed a lock wall at the Soo. The steamer just seemed to have occasional bouts of bad luck.

After probing into the circumstances of the STEIN-BRENNER loss, including interviewing all of the surviving crew, the Coast Guard Marine Board of Investigation concluded that "cause of the STEINBRENNER's foundering was heavy seas dislodging the three hatch covers nos. 10, 11 and 12 and permitting flooding of the cargo holds. The adverse weather conditions with mountainous seas combined to make this foundering an "act of God."

Without a doubt the Board felt the STEINBRENNER was seaworthy as evidenced by the American Bureau of Shipping endorsement of the load line certificate and the issuance of midsummer draft certificate on May 4, 1953. The steamer had been dry-docked February 11 - 20, 1953 at Buffalo for her five year survey for class and passed. She also passed her Coast Guard annual inspection. Captain Stiglin testified to the Board that when he had been in earlier blows that spring loaded with grain, coal and light, seas were taken aboard with the steamer without experiencing any trouble.

The Board looked closely at the question of the stripped threads on the hatch clamps and concluded that news stories concerning them were greatly exaggerated. One of the survivors, Kenneth L. Kumm, testified that when wrapped with marlin they drew up as tightly as the others. Although the Board considered Kumm short on sailing experience, they felt he was one of the most reliable and level-headed men testifying.

The Board also said there was no evidence to indicate that any of the stripped threads were on clamps on the after three hatches, the hatches the Board concluded actually caused the foundering.

How then did the hatch covers on hatches 10, 11 and 12 loosen and come free? The Board felt the working of the vessel in the heavy sea, with metal clamps drawn tight on metal hatch covers caused a general loosening of all the clamps. The heavy seas finished the job by knocking over the loosened clamps. Unsecured, the hatch covers came free.

In the Boards' opinion, the use of tarpaulins would have served to reduce the general working and loosening of the clamps, and helped prevent the free entry of water between the hatch leaves.

Strangely though, the Board did not blame Captain Stiglin for failing to secure his hatches with the tarpaulins. They felt that the same judgement would have been used by any reasonably prudent master under the same conditions, with erroneous weather forecasts. Not battening down while underway was just a case of an experienced seaman underestimating the force of the sea.

The no. 2 lifeboat was not properly launched thought the Board, simply due to panic. The crew realized with horror that the STEINBRENNER was indeed sinking and none were thinking too clearly. Contrary to the normal drill procedures, no man on the boat deck took charge of the lifeboat launching and confusion reigned.

After deliberations, the Board determined that there was "no evidence that any licensed or certified personnel of the vessel committed any act of incompetence, inattention to duty or negligence of willfull violation of any law or regulation." Neither did any personnel of the Coast Guard of any other government agency contribute to it. However, they felt the use of tarpaulins over the hatches would have prevented the casualty.

But the Commandant of the Coast Guard reviewed the Board's work and. . .disagreed! He felt that the STEINBRENNER was not lost due to an "act of God." Didn't the Board state that had the tarps been fitted over the hatches the STEINBRENNER would not have been lost? God had no business being blamed for human error.

Failure to fit the tarps was clearly against the Coast Guard regulations. "It should be the responsibility of the master to assure himself before leaving protected waters that all exposed cargo hatches of all his vessel are closed and made properly tight." Failure to comply with this regulation largely contributed to the vessel's loss. Accordingly action was initiated against the license of the master.

And so ends the story of the loss of the steamer HENRY STEINBRENNER and the death of 17 of her crew. The reason for the sinking is not found in the easy excuse of fate, but rather is the simple fact that the ship had not been prepared to face the sea condition met. Her hatch tarps had not been fitted and without them when the heavy weather struck the STEINBRENNER was lost, while other vessels larger or more properly prepared, survived.

FOOTNOTES

1. "EVENING NEWS" (Sault St. Marie) May 31, 1953.

2. In 1941 the 250 foot STEEL VENDOR sank in heavy seas off Manitou Island.

3. The "telephone booth" was really a long narrow tool room used for the storage of many items, including life jackets. A telephone was located for communication between the engineroom and the bridge.

BIBLIOGRAPHY

Annual Report. Lake Carriers Association, 1953.

Correspondence, Criminal Division, U.S. Department of Justice, December 20, 1973, July 29, 1977.

Doner, Mary Francis, "THE SALVAGER" Minneapolis: Ross & Haines, Inc., 1958.

"DULUTH NEWS-TRIBUNE" - May 11, 12, 13, 14, 15, 16, 17, 19, 1953.

"FORT WILLIAM DAILY TIMES-JOURNAL." May 11, 12, 13, 14, 15, 16, 1953.

Interview with Mr. Allen Augsburger, Valmy WI, March 11, 1978, survivor of the wreck of the HENRY STEINBRENNER.

Interview with Mr. Kenneth Kumm, Oxnard, CA, survivor of the HENRY STEINBRENNER.

"INLAND SEAS," winter, 1954.

Marine Board of Investigation: "FOUNDERING OF THE SS HENRY STEINBRENNER, MAY 11, 1953" U.S. Coast Guard.

"MERCHANT VESSELS OF THE U.S." Department of Transportation, U.S. Coast Guard, Government Printing Office, various issues.

"MILWAUKEE JOURNAL," May 11, 12, 13, 14, 1953.

"NEW YORK TIMES," May 12, August 7, 1953.

"EVENING NEWS" (Sault St. Marie, MI), May 11, 12, 13, 14, 15, 16, 17, 19, 1953.

"SKILLINGS MINING REVIEW," May 16, 1953.

Wolff, Julius F. "100 Years of Rescue, the Coast Guard on Lake Superior," "INLAND SEAS," spring, 1976.

SCOTIADOC

The 416 foot steamer SCOTIADOC.

A pea soup Lake Superior fog combined with a 55 mph gale spelled death for the 416 foot, 4,635 ton Canada Steamship Lines freighter SCOTIADOC. Outbound for Fort William on June 20, 1953 with a cargo of 253,000 bushels of wheat, she was rammed midships portside by the 444 foot steamer BURLINGTON at 5:57 in the afternoon. The fatal collision occurred approximately 3½ miles off Trowbridge Island, at the entrance to Thunder Bay. Within 30 minutes the SCOTIADOC had sunk in 82 fathoms. Standing by the stricken steamer, the BUR-LINGTON rescued 28 survivors. One man was lost when a lifeboat overturned while being lowered. The SCOTIA-DOC was a loss of $500,000.

The SCOTIADOC was built at Cleveland in 1904 by the American Shipbuilding Company for Hutchinsons's Buckeye Steamship Company. Originally named the MARTIN MULLEN, she was sold in October 1947 to the N.M. Patterson Company. Her new owner renamed her the SCOTIADOC. Patterson had the tradition of naming their ships after Canadian provinces and cities. The suffix DOC refers to "Dominion of Canada," while the prefix refers to Nova Scotia.

In the case of the SCOTIADOC, the question of "what's in a name" could have an interesting answer. Seven earlier ships named for Nova Scotia were lost; the first "lost at Cuba" in 1846; the second off South Carolina in 1911; the third off North Carolina in 1918; a fourth burning at Nova Scotia in 1921; the fifth foundering off Kodiak, Alaska in 1927; the sixth sinking off Pentwater, Michigan in 1940 and the last foundering in the Atlantic off Maine in March of 1947.

BIBLIOGRAPHY

"ANNUAL REPORT OF THE LAKE CARRIERS ASSOCIATION," 1953.
"Great Lakes Calendar." "INLAND SEAS." Fall, 1953.
"MINING JOURNAL" (Marquette), June 20, 22, 1953.
VanderLinden, Rev. Peter. "GREAT LAKES SHIPS WE REMEMBER." Cleveland: Freshwater Press, 1979.

INSHORE WRECKS

Many vessels have been either total losses or have suffered damages while navigating the inshore waters of Isle Royale. Some of these incidents were of major interest, such as the vessels preceding. Others were not quite as important, and the following list is an attempt to give the reader an appreciation of the type of minor incident which frequently occurred in and around Isle Royale. I have not included the wrecks of miscellaneous cabin cruisers and pleasure craft.

SISKAWIT

In October 1840, this small schooner of the American Fur Company stranded on a reef off the present day Fisherman's Home. The next spring she was hauled free by the famous schooner JOHN JACOB ASTOR and the legendary Captain Charles Stannard.

The SISKAWIT was later wrecked off Marquette's Chocolay River on Christmas Day, 1849. She was trying to enter the river for winter lay-up when the mishap occurred.

LAMPLIGHTER

This 120-ton schooner stranded off Isle Royale on September 11, 1857. The tug OSWEGO successfully hauled her off and towed her to Detroit for repairs. The 11th Lighthouse District Inspector reported the accident was caused by the "neglect of duty of Captain Taylor, Master of the Supply Vessel." The LAMPLIGHTER, originally built as the CHALLENGE, had been purchased by the U.S. Lighthouse Board in May 1856 for $6,250.

YOU TELL

September 26, 1872 proved to be a black day for the schooner YOU TELL of Duluth. Caught in a north blow, she struck the rocks near Washington Harbor, becoming a total loss of $3,100. A year earlier, the schooner had been dismasted in a gale, perhaps an omen of things to come.

LITTLE WILL

On June 24, 1876, this small steamer became lost while enroute to Port Arthur and in attempting to land at the Menagerie Island Light, lost her rudder. After a four hour search, the light-keeper found the rudder, shipped it and giving the steamer directions, got her on her way.

The NORTHERN QUEEN, a victim of the dreaded Rock of Ages Reef.

Courtesy C. Patrick Labadie

NORTHERN BELLE

A small 40-foot schooner reported abandoned near Malone Bay, circa 1885.

GOLDEN EAGLE

A vessel stranded at Isle Royale in 1892.

JOHN JEWETT

A 92-foot schooner that stranded in Grace Harbor on October 7, 1898.

OSCEOLA

During a heavy gale on November 21, 1898, the small wooden steamer OSCEOLA was blown ashore on a reef off Mott Island. She was only able to free herself after jettisoning 2,000 barrels of her salt cargo. Thus for a short time, Superior was "salty".

The OSCEOLA, 183 feet in length and 980 gross tons, was built by F.W. Wheeler at Bay City, Michigan in 1882 for the Crescent Transportation Company. In 1905 she was sold Canadian and renamed GOLSPIE. On December 7, 1906, she was wrecked at Brule Bay, Lake Superior.

NORTHERN QUEEN

Poor visibility on September 10, 1913 accounted for another Rock of Ages wreck when the 300 foot steel steamer plowed into an outlying reef three-quarters of a mile south from the light. Considerably damaged, the vessel required the best efforts of the Port Arthur tugs JAMES WHALEN and J.T. HORNE with the barge EMPIRE. Bottom damages were extensive, resulting in a $22,500 repair bill.

WILLIAM T. ROBERTS

As shown in so many other accounts, fog around Isle Royale has often befuddled shipmasters. The 504 foot WILLIAM T. ROBERTS was a typical example. On May 1, 1917, she ran up on a reef in a pea souper necessitating extensive bottom plate replacement.

W.G. POLLOCK

Navigation near Rock of Ages Reef has always been a bit tricky. On November 15, 1923, while steaming past Rock of Ages, the steel steamer W.G. POLLOCK struck what was only identified as a "submerged object," but judging from the damages, a broken propeller tail shaft, wheel and hub, a damaged rudder and shoe, and four engine columns broken off, it must have been a rock reef! Damages were estimated at $22,000.

PETER A.B. WIDNENER

Rock of Ages Reef tore up another wreck on November 17, 1926. Driven by storm lashed seas, the 580 foot freighter PETER A.B. WIDNENER "floated" over part of the reef tearing off its rudder and rendering her uncontrollable. Drifting before the storm the strong northeasterner battered her for a day before she was taken in tow off Duluth. Damages were placed at $4,000.

DAGMAR

The small 14 ton gas powered fish tug DAGMAR sank at Isle Royale on June 1, 1935.

PC 782

An embarrassment to the U.S. Navy occurred on May 28, 1949 when PC 782, a Naval Reserve training ship, ran hard on a reef in Siskiwit Bay. Based in Duluth, the vessel was on a weekend training cruise. Since the weather was calm and clear, there was no apparent reason for the accident. It took a fleet of vessels, including the Coast Guard Cutters WOODRUSH and MESQUITE, the icebreaker MACKINAW, a Corps of Engineers tug, the dredge-barge FAITH, complete with a 90 ton crane, another Naval Reserve training ship and wrecking tug FAVORITE to haul her free. Extensive repairs were later made in Duluth.

OFF SHORE WRECKS

The offshore waters of Lake Superior have long been infamous in the Saga of Great Lakes shipwrecks. The waters off Isle Royale are no exception. Many a fine vessel met her end when caught in the hoary hands of fate while in an area that could roughly be described as "off Isle Royale." The following list is a partial compilation of those vessels.

CELT

One of the smaller vessel losses in the vicinity of Isle Royale occurred on August 18, 1889 when the pleasure yacht CELT sank 15 miles south of Siskiwit Harbor. The yacht had sprung a leak, giving those aboard only a very short time to launch the yawlboat. They spent several days on the lake until the steamer SAMUEL MATHER spotted the survivors and brought them to the Soo.

MONROE C. SMITH

The MONROE C. SMITH, a 380 foot steamer that went on the rocks at Passage Island on May 16, 1917, was enroute from Fort William to Buffalo with wheat. She released herself without help and returned to Port Arthur. Damages were placed at $8,000.

FERDINAND SCHLESINGER

May 26, 1919 saw the loss of the 305-foot, 2,607 ton wooden steamer FERDINAND SCHLESINGER. The steamer was upbound for Port Arthur with a cargo of

2,000 tons of coal when she began to leak heavily. Regardless of the efforts of the engineers, her pumps were unable to expel the great gulps of water the steamer was swallowing. At 5:50 a.m., while 15 miles southeast of Passage Island, the SCHLESINGER sank. The crew was picked up by the steamer ASSINBOIA, which happened on the scene just before the steamer sank.

The SCHLESINGER was one of the largest wooden steamers ever built. When launched in 1891, she was only the second wooden bulk freighter built with a compartmentized double bottom. Such a unique bottom was used to pump water ballast into. Normally, such a special bottom was reserved only for steel hulled vessels.

The FERDINAND SCHLESINGER on the way down.

Archives, Michigan Department of State

F.B. SQUIRE

On April 22, 1919, the 410-foot steel steamer F.B. SQUIRE ran over a Passage Island reef. Damages were estimated at $25,000. She was bound out from Fort William for Buffalo with grain. The weather was clear and it was thought she struck an unchartered shoal.

LUZON

During a typical Isle Royale fog, the 346-foot steamer LUZON rammed hard on the rocks of Passage Island on October 7, 1923. She was recovered, but with a considerable repair cost.

We at *Avery Color Studios* thank you for purchasing this book. We hope it has provided many hours of enjoyable reading.

Learn more about Michigan and the Great Lakes area through a broad range of titles that cover mining and logging days, early Indians and their legends, Great Lakes shipwrecks, Cully Gage's Northwoods Readers (full of laughter and occasional sadness), and full-color pictorials of days gone by and the natural beauty of this land.

Also available are beautiful full-color placemats and note stationery.

To obtain a free catalog, please call (800) 722-9925 in Michigan, or (906) 892-8251, or tear out this page and mail it to us. Please tape or staple the card and put a stamp on it.

PLEASE RETURN TO:

Avery **Color Studios**
Star Route - Box 275
Au Train, Michigan 49806
Phone: (906) 892-8251
IN MICHIGAN
CALL TOLL FREE
1-800-722-9925

Your complete shipping address:

_____

_____

_____

_____

Fold, Staple, Affix Stamp and Mail

_____

_____

_____

_____

Avery COLOR STUDIOS
Star Route - Box 275
AuTrain, Michigan 49806